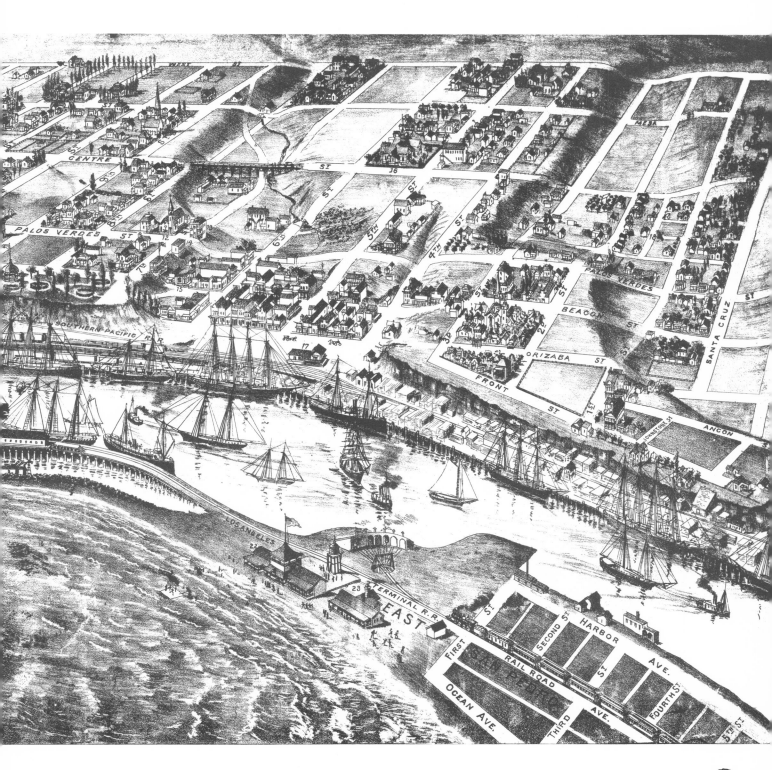

17. **S.P. DEPOT**
18. **PARADISE VALLEY**
19. **EPISCOPAL CHURCH**
20. **SAN PEDRO LUMBER CO. MILLS (not shown)**
21. **L.A. TERMINAL DEPOT AND WHARF**
22. **L.A. TERMINAL BATHHOUSE**
23. **L.A. TERMINAL PAVILION**
24. **DEADMAN'S ISLAND**

Tenth Anniversary
Commemorative Edition

June 1985

Congratulations on having such wonderful children—!

(But then we had wonderful parents !!)

Rebekah Janelle

Marky

Paul

Cheryl Kathleen

Elizabeth

Pacific Northwest

Gardener's Almanac

The Complete How-to Book for the Vegetable Grower

by *Mary Kenady*

Master Gardener

▷ **Groundwork:** how to analyze your soil and make it better — pH, organic matter and where to get it, composting, fertilizer, earthworms . . .

▷ **Conditioning:** getting rid of unwanted growth, digging, weeding, mulching, watering, tools . . .

▷ **Planting:** where, when, how; single rows, wide rows, raised beds, blocks; seeds or sets, crop rotation, intensive planting, companion planting . . .

▷ **Extending the season:** greenhouses, coldframes, hotbeds, plastic cloches, tunnels, ground cover; starting seeds, winter gardening . . .

▷ **Pests and problems:** insects, diseases, weeds, marauders . . .

▷ How experts garden from southern Oregon to southern British Columbia, the Pacific Coast to the western Rockies . . .

▷ Plus weather data, vegetables that mature in your climate, best varieties, where to get seeds and starts, how to harvest, how to store, where to go for help . . .

San Pedro
A PICTORIAL HISTORY

MORETON BAY FIG TREE AND POINT FERMIN LIGHTHOUSE

San Pedro
a pictorial history

Henry P. Silka

Picture Captions:
    Irene M. Almeida, editor
    Flora Twyman Baker
    William L. Olesen
    Kathryn Schultz

assisted by:
    Arthur A. Almeida
    Samuel Botwin

San Pedro Bay Historical Society

Book Design and Editorial Consultation: Dan Healy

Jacket Design and Illustration: Judy Ferguson

Text Illustrations: Ingrid Tostrup

Typesetting: Entropy Enterprises

Library of Congress Catalog Card Number: 84-51422

ISBN: 0-9611556-1-2

CONTENTS

Am I the only one who remembers?

At the end of Centre Street, steps going down to a bath-house and a fine beach.

The South Coast Yacht Club on the bluff at Twenty-first Street and the steps going down to the pier.

The Van Camp Cannery at the north end of the Southern Pacific slip, not far from the location of the hotel at Timms Point.

The two ferry boats, one going to Terminal Island and the other to East San Pedro. The wonderful picnic grounds, the dance pavilion, the boardwalk and beautiful homes, and how the ferry got stuck in the mud and had to wait for the tide to come in.

And Point Fermin Park with steps and paths going down to the beach, and the tide pools and the dance pavilion at the west end of the park, the bandstand and the covered swimming pool and playgrounds.

Downtown San Pedro: Beacon Street with stores and banks and theatres and sweet shops, and the fine people who owned them and the people who worked there.

The Angelus Hotel on Fourth and Centre Streets, owned by Mr. and Mrs. Norby, and the Fifth Street Auditorium.

And White Point when there was just a path to go down to the beach, and the Japanese were in the business of drying abalones and the swimming pool that was destroyed by a storm.

The Royal Palms Golf Club with the club house built on the bluff and the golf course that is now lower South Shores. And the evenings we spent dancing at Royal Palms. How the club had beautified the hill with paths and stone benches and lovely plants. And how we watched the club house burn down in 1955, set afire by two boys.

And how happy I am that San Pedro is my home.

GLADYS NORMAN KOPP

ACKNOWLEDGEMENTS

The San Pedro Bay Historical Society is indebted to many of its members and to numerous friends who have assisted in the compilation of this local history. The genesis of this work came about through a $1,000 grant from the San Pedro branch of the 1976 Los Angeles National Bicentennial Committee.

Henry P. Silka chaired the original (1976) committee which researched and collected historical data on San Pedro. In 1980 Society President Arthur A. Almeida reactivated an expanded Publication Committee that was chaired by J. Peter Mandia. Silka soon submitted the first drafts and outlines of an official history, and the group met at intervals to discuss and make suggestions as the text progressed. Due to other society needs taking precedence, work on the book was temporarily discontinued.

In 1982 Irene M. Almeida headed an Editorial Committee composed of A. Almeida, Flora Twyman Baker, Frances and Samuel Botwin, Everett G. Hager, Harold Jones, William L. Olesen, Curtis Sheffield and Kathryn Schultz. This group made recommendations and reviewed Silka's text. The society especially acknowledges the members of the Caption Subcommittee, who gave so generously of their time and extraordinary talents. This group consisting of I. Almeida, F. Baker, W. Olesen and K. Schultz, with assistance from A. Almeida, S. Botwin and H. Silka, selected the graphics and photos that enliven this work and wrote the captions.

The support staff included: Robert A. Schultz, finances; Robert Bentovoja, technical assistance; Lourette Almeida, Avanell Farrell, Karen Hardin and Gayle Williamson, typists.

We are fortunate to have special drawings by local artist Ingrid Tostrup, whose illustrations are featured in chapter one and whose display initials introduce each chapter. Anna Marie and E.G. Hager lent their professional expertise to the demanding task of compiling the index of this volume. Agrex Inc. and the office of Councilwoman Joan Milke Flores provided special services. It is with warm gratitude that the society commends all the foregoing groups and individuals for their efforts and contributions.

We are grateful to Pamela Bleich, Betty Buzzini, Anna (Hughes) Craig, Lt. Col. A. David Gustafson, A. M. Hager, Hilda Hager, Arthur Hendrickson, Grace Hoxworth, Elizabeth McKinney, Ralph Preciado and Marian Skidmore, who served on one or more of the previous committees and assembled the necessary preparatory research.

Our heartfelt thanks are extended to the many organizations and individuals who provided the pictures that augmented those from the society's archives: Cabrillo Marine Museum, the Herbert Peck Culler Collection, the Fire Belles, Huntington Library, Los Angeles Harbor Department, Los Angeles Maritime Museum, *Palos Verdes Peninsula News*, the Fay Pesutich Collection, San Pedro *News-Pilot*, Security Pacific National Bank Photograph Collection, Los Angeles Public Library, Southwest Museum, Title Insurance and Trust Company, Todd Pacific Shipyard, the Vincent Thomas Collection, Union Oil Company of California, University of California at Los Angeles and the Robert Weinstein Collection.

Individual contributors include: A. Almeida, Kate Acuna, Audrey Bacon, F. Baker, Robert Beck, F. and S. Botwin, Tom Coulter, Charles Ember, Ida Frumes, Donald M. Gales, Dr. L.C. and Angela Garvey, Charles E. Goodman, A. M. and E.G. Hager, Ford M. Harris, Edward Hauck, Lynn Husted Hopkins, Jack Hunter, Mas Ishibashi, Frank Keeler, Tim Lemm, Michael P. Levitt, Rudecinda Lo Buglio, Kenneth Malloy, P. Mandia, Mike Markulis, Felix Medina, David Miner, Lupe Munoz, W. Olesen, John Olguin, Allan Pike, Tim I. Purdy, Mr. and Mrs. James Robb, Bob Sachs, K. Schultz, Sumi Seo Seki, Jackie Shellhart, Mary Thomas, Dr. and Mrs. Anthony Turhollow, Howard Uller, Earl Waggoner and H. D. Weddle.

Union Oil Company of California granted the society $5,000, which ensured the publication of this book. We are appreciative of their concern for the preservation of San Pedro's history and for their continuing philanthropic contributions to the community. Our gratitude is also extended to A. Almeida for his fund-raising efforts and to Congressman Glenn M. Anderson and Kimball Hill for their special assistance in acquiring this grant.

This publication has been wrought with love and the desire to preserve the rich heritage and history of the community of San Pedro. Because this has been a committee project, or more properly, the project of several committees, it has taken more time to complete than originally anticipated. The result, however, is the product of a thorough review of available materials, intensive research and preparation that is representative of the society.

Posing before the so-called Danish Castle is the Editorial Committee: Irene (editor) and Arthur Almeida, Frances and Samuel Botwin, Kathryn and Robert Schultz, William Olesen, Flora Baker, Curtis Sheffield and Everett Hager.

Many thanks to Henry Silka for his dedication to this project. As an historian by avocation, though residing outside of the area, his perspective is wide, yet no less accurate. The result is a concise, chronological presentation, which acquaints the reader with all the salient points.

Finally, our gratitude to all who down through the years have contributed to the preservation of the memories, history and treasured mementos of this community and its unique harbor.

THE EDITORIAL COMMITTEE

1

San Pedro.   California

BEFORE THE 'YANQUIS'

**A**T LEAST SIX INDIAN VILLAGES flourished near the shore when Juan Rodriguez Cabrillo sailed into San Pedro Bay in October, 1542, on a voyage of exploration for the Viceroy of New Spain. Cabrillo, a Portuguese in the service of Spain, named these waters *Bahia de los Fumos* ("Bay of Smokes"). The source of the smoke is not definitely known. It has been said that the haze came from dying signal fires that had burned the previous night to guide returning fishing parties. Others suggested that the smoke came from grass fires set by the Indians during one of their rabbit drives.

Cabrillo's ships departed the next day. There is no evidence to prove conclusively that Cabrillo or any of his men actually set foot on shore. The Spaniards did not remain on the California coast long enough to upset the established pattern of Indian life. Except for a brief visit in 1602 by the Spanish exploration party under Sebastian Vizcaino, there were no other foreign intrusions until the late 1700s. Vizcaino's survey data resulted in the confusion of two new names for Cabrillo's *Bahia de los Fumos*. The bay was referred to as *San Pedro*, in honor of Saint Peter, Bishop of Alexandria, and *Ensenada de San Andres*, in honor of Saint Andrew. It was the custom of Spanish explorers to name a discovery for the saint's day of the Catholic calendar on which it occurred. Apparently, there was confusion for many years concerning the particular saint's day on which Vizcaino visited San Pedro Bay. However, in his 1734 description of Vizcaino's voyage, cosmographer Cabrera Bueno called it San Pedro Bay and this has been the official name ever since.

Knowledge of Indian life comes to us through recorded eyewitness accounts and through the study of archeological evidence. There were probably as many as ten villages on the whole of the Palos Verdes Peninsula. These were located along the coast from the hills overlooking today's Harbor Lake to Malaga Cove. Villages were usually made up of related families that formed a large clan

Opposite page: **1842. William Meyers' watercolor is the earliest known depiction of San Pedro. Note only one structure is visible, the trading post Casa de San Pedro.**

Coastal Indians of the Shoshonean tribe were ingenious in devising means for storing precious water. Illustrated is a water bottle constructed of reeds lined with waterproofing asphaltum and decorated with an inlay of shell beads.

Indian homes were constructed of tules over a framework of branches. This is a representation of the Indian life diorama by Elizabeth Mason at Southwest Museum.

or several smaller clans. The coastal villages were generally larger than those inland, some having populations exceeding 300 people. Living in domed, circular houses constructed of slender willow poles thatched with grass and rushes, the Indians subsisted on fish, shellfish, cactus fruit, berries, seeds, deer, antelope, small game and waterfowl. They augmented their diet with acorns and seeds received from inland villages, for which they traded seafood.

Though considered generally peaceful, the Indians did have wars. Three or four blood-related villages commonly allied themselves against other villages similarly associated and everyone became involved. The old men followed the young warriors while the women and children trailed in the rear. The wars seem to have been bloody affairs in which no warriors were taken prisoner: the wounded were decapitated where they had fallen, and slaves were made of captured women and children. However, these bloody combats were apparently less frequent than "song fights" where the people of opposing villages squared off to sing insulting and obscene songs at each other.

A large and important village was situated on the side of the hill above what is now Anaheim Street between the Harbor Freeway and Gaffey Street, where the Union Oil Company refinery is located. This was Suang-na, "Place of the Rushes." Portions of the village were still inhabited in the 1850s. In those days the lake in what is now Harbor Park was called Machado Lake, and later Bixby Slough. During seasons of heavy rainfall, the entire lowland area became a huge marsh. With this source of abundant fresh water, building materials, fish and game, Suang-na was a prosper-

HERRING GULL

BLACK-BACKED GULL

GRAY SEAL

DIAMOND-BACK RATTLER

HARBOR SEAL

BLACK-TAIL JACKRABBIT

ous village. Also adding to the village's importance and prosperity was its proximity to a crossing of major Indian trails, which today is the intersection of Gaffey and Anaheim Streets, Vermont Avenue and Palos Verdes Drive North, commonly called Five Points. Other villages were located in San Pedro. Archeological evidence places a village near Channel and Gaffey Streets and another at Gaffey and Twenty-third Streets. Other villages are suspected to have existed at various points along the beach and the bluff lining the west shore of the bay, and also on the seacoast at White Point.

Unfortunately, the Indians were not totally insulated from the events of the larger world, which permanently intruded upon their lives when Spanish authorities decreed that Alta California should be settled by the subjects of Spain. Starting with the establishment of the presidio and mission at San Diego in 1769, missionaries, soldiers and settlers came up from Mexico to establish outposts of the Spanish empire throughout the length of California. In 1771 San Gabriel Mission was founded and the Indians of the Palos Verdes Peninsula became the wards of these mission fathers. Thereafter, they were known as the Gabrielino Indians. Ten years later a secular community was established: *el Pueblo de Nuestra Señora la Reina de Los Angeles de Porciuncula.* The stage was set for the permanent displacement of the Indians and their culture.

Animal, marine, plant and bird life, the available resources of this area, provided not only food for the Indians but clothing, shelter and materials for the creation of implements, ornaments and even what could be regarded as luxuries.

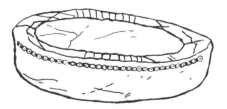

Archeological digs in the peninsula area have uncovered items of exceptional beauty such as the steatite bowl decorated with small white shells set in asphaltum.

In 1784 Juan Jose Dominguez, a retired leather-jacket soldier of Spain, drove his horses and a small herd of cattle onto the grasslands south of the pueblo. Pedro Fages, his one-time military commander and now the governor of Alta California, had granted him grazing rights to about 75,000 acres. On this land the old soldier started Rancho San Pedro, one of the first major ranchos of Spanish California. He considered that his grant included all of Palos Verdes Peninsula and present day Redondo Beach, with an eastern boundary that generally followed the course of the Los Angeles River as it flows today. (The San Gabriel River flowed in that channel in Juan Jose's time.) He placed his northernmost limit at the boundary of the pueblo's communal grazing land (about where Rosecrans Avenue is today). In all, he claimed rights to approximately 115 square miles. During the subsequent 200 years some of today's South Bay communities, the Harbor District of Los Angeles, Compton, Carson and part of Long Beach were to be carved out of this acreage.

Juan Jose died in 1809 after an illness of many years. He had been a bachelor and left no direct descendants who were recognized as legal heirs. His nephew Cristobal Dominguez, a soldier stationed at San Juan Capistrano, assumed the rights of inheritance to the rancho. As Cristobal could not leave his military post, Rancho San Pedro was left in the care of Manuel Gutierrez, executor of the old soldier's will. Gutierrez had managed the ranch during the years of Juan Jose's illness and had grazing rights that had been given to him by the deceased. His own cattle numbered over 9,000 head, and during the long years of his management of the rancho, Gutierrez assumed rights of ownership, which grew stronger as Cristobal delayed taking personal charge of his inheritance.

In 1810 Gutierrez granted grazing rights to a seventeen-year-old soldier, Jose Dolores Sepulveda (possibly a relative). Young Jose Dolores worked diligently in building up his stake and called it Rancho de los Palos Verdes. However, his holdings were threatened when Cristobal Dominguez finally took action to claim his inheritance. In 1817 Cristobal petitioned Governor Pablo Sola to confirm his rights to Rancho San Pedro and to order all unauthorized parties to vacate. The governor ruled in his favor, but Jose Dolores remained on the ranch in defiance and Cristobal failed to take immediate steps to remove him.

Mexico proclaimed her independence from Spain in 1822. That year Cristobal again petitioned Governor Sola. Being past sixty and in poor health, he sent his nineteen-year-old son, Manuel Dominguez, to plead this case with the governor. Another decree ordering the Sepulvedas to vacate was issued. By this time Jose

Dolores had built a home* for his family of six children and had increased his herd to over 800 head of cattle. He was firm in the belief that he had legal right to Rancho de los Palos Verdes, and that the boundaries of the property extended from about where Sepulveda Boulevard is today on the north, Figueroa Street and the harbor on the east, and the Pacific Ocean on the south and west, about 32,000 acres in all.

In 1824 Jose Dolores traveled to Monterey and personally presented his petition to the new governor, Luis Arguello. On the return journey he was killed when Indians attacked Mission de la Purisima Concepcion, where he was spending the night. He left a baby girl, Maria Teresa, and four boys: Juan Capistrano (Juan), Ygnacio, Jose Diego (Diego) and Jose Loreto (Jose). The next year his widow married Antonio Machado, who had also received permission from Gutierrez to run cattle on the land. For a while neither party in the controversy took further action.

Cristobal Dominguez died in January, 1825. In the spring his son Manuel, now twenty-two, moved the Dominguez family from San Juan Capistrano. His mother and two sisters lived in the pueblo while Manuel and two younger brothers moved into a crude adobe ranch house built years before by old Juan Jose. Slowly, they developed the ranch, building the original wing of the Dominguez Ranch Adobe that is still standing today. To this house he brought his bride, Maria Engracia de Cota of neighboring Rancho los Cerritos, after they married in 1827. Meanwhile, Manuel had continued his appeals and had obtained two decrees from Governor Jose Maria Echeandia ordering the Sepulvedas and Machados to vacate the land. But to Manuel's consternation, this same governor, acting on Machado's petition, provisionally granted Rancho de los Palos Verdes to the Sepulvedas.

The controversy was to continue for the next nineteen years. During this time, the older Sepulveda boys married and built homes. Juan's was near the present intersection of Gaffey and Anaheim Streets, which generally paralleled old Indian trails. Jose Loreto's home was located farther south, about where Capitol Drive is now, and somewhat west of Gaffey Street. No traces of their homes survive. Finally, in 1846 Governor Pio Pico confirmed the Sepulvedas in their right to Rancho de los Palos Verdes. In issuing his grant he set aside 500 varas square (41.2 acres) for public access

*California Historical Landmark No. 383. The exact site of this home built in 1818 is not known. Report No. 27 of the California Department of Natural Resources and State Parks Commission states: "East of Walteria at the foot of Palos Verdes Hills, Madison Street runs into the canyon in which are located the pits of the Dicalite Co., Los Angeles County."

in the area of the bluff that had come into use as an embarcadero. The Middle Reservation of Fort MacArthur was later built on that land.

During the whole period of litigation, commerce and world trade were expanding at San Pedro Harbor. Under Spanish rule foreign vessels had been prohibited from trading directly at any California port except Monterey. The annual supply ship sailed from San Blas, Mexico, and delivered its cargo to the presidios from where it was distributed to the missions and pueblos. The single authorized supply ship had been insufficient for the needs of the growing California population. To their further distress, there had been years in which there were no supply ships at all. So when the American brig *Lelia Byrd* put into the bay in 1805, the Americans found a ready market for the European-manufactured articles and oriental luxuries carried in the vessel's hold. They traded these for cattle hides and sea otter pelts. Other vessels followed over the years and a clandestine trade was carried on, but it was not until after Mexican independence that California ports were officially opened to foreign trade.

Two Englishmen working for a trading company in Lima, Peru, were quick to take advantage. In 1822 Hugh McCulloch and William Hartnell started the firm of McCulloch, Hartnell and Company to trade in California hides and tallow, with the hides destined for England and the tallow for Peru. They succeeded in contracting with the missions for cattle hides at one peso each and tallow at two pesos an *arroba* (about twenty-five pounds). The company was permitted to build warehouses at Monterey and San Pedro. In 1823 they built an adobe structure* measuring about twenty-by-fifty feet on the bluff where the Middle Reservation of Fort MacArthur now stands. Hardly had McCulloch and Hartnell concluded their

*California Historical Landmark No. 920. A plaque sponsored by the San Pedro Bay Historical Society and placed just east of the Fort MacArthur Parade Ground in 1979 marks the site.

1855. The Hide House, described by Richard Henry Dana in 1835 as a single adobe structure, was built by the firm of Hartnell and McCulloch in 1823 for trade activity with the Missions San Fernando and San Gabriel. This was the first known commercial structure on San Pedro Bay and marked the start of today's great Port of Los Angeles. The illustration by Lieutenant J. M. Alden shows expansion of the facility after the American occupation. A marker indicating the exact location of the original structure is near the eastern edge of the Fort MacArthur Parade Ground.

deal when ships from Boston began to call regularly for hides. The decade of the 1820s saw a steady growth in the hide trade that came to be dominated by Yankee traders.

San Pedro was not a safe harbor. Alfred Robinson, who came here for hides in 1828, wrote: "The harbor of St. Pedro is an extensive bay, and, although not considered a safe anchorage during the winter months, when the southeast wind prevails, yet vessels frequently embark and discharge their cargoes here at all seasons of the year. The best anchorage is close under the northwest point of the bay, about three quarters of a mile outside of a small and rocky island [Deadman's Island*]; and the same distance from the beach. There is a house at the landing-place which generally serves as a land-mark . . . . From the month of October, til the beginning of May, vessels anchor at least a mile outside of these bearings, and ships are necessarily prepared for slipping their cables, and getting under way, should the wind, as is often the case, chop in suddenly from the S.E."**

Captains dared not anchor their vessels closer lest a sudden southeaster blow them upon the shore. Cargo was unloaded into the ships' boats and rowed to shore. The boats brought back hides and tallow for loading into the ship. Yet the shipmasters braved the dangers for by this time the Pueblo of Los Angeles was the largest settlement in California, with a population of about 1,000.

McCulloch and Hartnell suffered a series of financial reverses and dissolved their partnership. In 1829 the hide warehouse was sold to the San Gabriel Mission. Upon secularization of the mission five years later, ownership of the Hide House was acquired by Abel Stearns, a New England Yankee who had established himself in business at the pueblo. Stearns renovated and enlarged the building and it became an important branch of his trading business. On three occasions he was accused of smuggling to avoid the high import-export duties imposed by the Mexican authorities. The Hide House came to be known as Casa de San Pedro and was often used as a mail drop by ships frequenting the California coast.

The hide business flourished through the 1830s, with over 100,000 hides said to have been shipped out of San Pedro alone. Yet, for all the activity in the bay, San Pedro remained largely uninhabited — the nearest dwelling being that of Jose Sepulveda, three miles away. Richard Henry Dana landed at San Pedro as a seaman aboard the Boston brig *Pilgrim* in 1835. He later described what he had seen: "The land was of a clayey consistency, and, as

*This small island was removed from the channel in the 1920s.

**Alfred Robinson, *Life in California*, pp. 37-38.

far as the eye could reach, entirely bare of trees and even shrubs, and there was no sign of a town, not even a house to be seen."* Supporting Dana's observations are the census records of 1836 and 1844 for the pueblo and surrounding ranches. The 1836 count reveals that seventy-five people lived on Rancho San Pedro, including the peninsula, while the 1844 count shows only twenty-eight people, excluding Indians in both cases.

As shipping activity increased, the Sepulvedas built a crude dock at a point just north of Stearns' Hide House. The Sepulveda Landing was located at the base of the bluff below where Fifteenth Street meets Beacon Street today. (Modern landfill operations to develop port facilities have pushed the bay away from the base of the bluff.) The Sepulvedas kept a *caballada* and supplied horses to arriving passengers and seamen for the long ride to the pueblo.

From Laurance L. Hill, *La Reina* (Los Angeles: Security Trust and Savings Bank, 1929).

Abel Stearns developed the Casa de San Pedro (Hide House) into a prosperous trading enterprise during the 1830s and 1840s. Amassing a fortune, he became one of the most influential men in Southern California. The establishment of San Pedro as a great port is due in part to his business activities. Stearns married Arcadia Bandini, daughter of Juan Bandini—a union that allied him with leading Californio families.

ABEL STEARNS   ARCADIA BANDINI STEARNS

Stearns sold the Hide House in 1845 to John Temple and David W. Alexander, two other Americans who were in business in Los Angeles. The next year 500 varas around the Hide House were set aside for public use when Governor Pico excluded the land from his grant of Rancho de los Palos Verdes to the Sepulvedas. This act officially recognized the area as public land and designated it for port activities. The year 1846 was fateful in yet another way: war broke out between Mexico and the United States and San Pedro was invaded.

*Richard Henry Dana, *Two Years Before the Mast*, p. 98.

Early in August the United States frigate *Congress* landed a force of sailors and marines at San Pedro. They marched on Los Angeles which offered no resistance. Leaving only a small contingent to occupy the pueblo, the naval force withdrew. At the end of September, however, the Californios revolted against the Americans, who were permitted to withdraw to San Pedro. Here they were eventually met by the American warship *Savannah*, which landed more men, and the combined force marched north to retake the pueblo. Near the Dominguez ranch house they encountered armed Californios, and after a brief battle in which they suffered some killed and wounded, the Americans retreated to their ship. The next morning four American dead were buried on *Isla de los Muertos* ("Deadman's Island"). By a clever ruse the Californios made it appear that their forces were larger than was actually the case and so the American units departed from San Pedro Bay.

The war in California finally ended in 1847 after the Battle of La Mesa, southeast of the pueblo. Ygnacio Sepulveda, one of the last casualties of the conflict, was killed in that battle. (During the conflict American forces had occupied the Hide House on the bluff. A document dated April 11, 1847, now in the Los Angeles City Archives, Office of City Clerk, reveals that the U.S. Government was liable for rent at a rate of fifty dollars per month beginning August 11, 1846. It is unclear whether said rent was ever paid.)

OCTOBER 1846. *American Marines execute an orderly retreat toward San Pedro during the Battle of Dominguez. The jubilant caballeros with the cannon at right have reason to rejoice, at least for the moment.*

2

THE ALDEN BESSE

THE AMERICAN INFLUX

THE AMERICAN FLAG replaced the Mexican flag over California. Manuel Dominguez went to Monterey in 1849 as a delegate to the Constitutional Convention. The gold rush was in full swing. Though the gold seekers bypassed Los Angeles on the way to the diggings in Northern California, the ranchos of the south did share in the economic benefits of the sudden population explosion. The rancheros drove cattle northward for sale to the camps that were springing up all over the mining country. But trouble was brewing for the landowners. Disappointed prospectors began drifting away from the gold fields. They squatted on the ranchos and clamored for land of their own to farm. Congress passed the Land Act of 1850, which was to prove fatal to the California rancheros for the act placed upon them the burden of proving valid title to their own land.

Both the Dominguez and Sepulveda families filed claims to their respective ranchos and both were confirmed in their titles by the Board of Land Commissioners. However, the board's actions were appealed in court, resulting in legal maneuvers that were to drag on for years. Manuel Dominguez successfully fought the challenges and received his patent for Rancho San Pedro in 1858. The Sepulveda brothers were not as fortunate and they came to be plagued by a series of lawsuits instigated from within as well as from outside the large Sepulveda family.

The year of the devastating land act also saw the granting of statehood to California. Immigration into the Los Angeles area was a mere trickle compared to the rush of humanity through the Golden Gate. San Francisco mushroomed into the Port of Entry for California and all imported goods destined for Los Angeles had to be transshipped from there, adding much to the cost. An important prerequisite for the economic development of Los Angeles was to have San Pedro designated a Port of Entry with its own custom house, so the good merchants of the pueblo petitioned Congress for that purpose. Among the documents in the Los Angeles City

Opposite page: **The bark ALDEN BESSE, built in 1871 at Bath, Maine, was originally used for world trade. Finally, decrepit and unseaworthy, she ended up as one of the first vessels used as a prop by the infant motion picture industry, circa 1910.**

CAPTAIN AUGUSTUS W. TIMMS   LOUISA THERESA TIMMS

1880. A German immigrant, Timms arrived in San Pedro, circa 1848, and quickly established himself in the lighterage and trade business. He acquired lands at waterside (Timms Landing), in the Vinegar Hill section, at Point Fermin and near the Government Reserve. He deeded the latter parcel to the City of San Pedro in 1888 for the cemetery, wherein he was buried later in the same year.

Archives is a copy of a letter dated May 27, 1850, from merchant John Temple to United States Senator Thomas Hart Benton of Missouri, a supporter of California development. The letter accompanied a petition to Congress "...in reference to making the Port of San Pedro (the port so called for this City) a Port of Entry."

In 1851 Phineas Banning, an enterprising young man of twenty-one, arrived at San Pedro. While clerking in a Baltimore counting house, he was hired to escort a cargo of merchandise to Los Angeles. The young man's energy and intelligence were quickly

DON JOSE DIEGO SEPULVEDA

MARIA FRANCISCA
ELIZALDE DE SEPULVEDA

Don Jose Diego Sepulveda, of the "San Pedro Sepulvedas," was born on Rancho de los Palos Verdes, circa 1820. He married Maria Francisca Elizalde on June 24, 1843. Three of their children — Roman, Aurelio and Rudecinda — survived to share in the partition of the property that comprises much of present-day San Pedro. A fourth share was divided between the daughters of Esperanza Sepulveda de Bandini: Arcadia Bandini de Gaffey and Dolores Bandini de Ward.

recognized and he was hired by David Douglass and William Sanford, Los Angeles merchants. Later, Banning went to work for David W. Alexander when that merchant dissolved his partnership with John Temple. Banning managed operations at the Hide House and aggressively competed for the business of hauling freight and passengers to Los Angeles. Within a short time he became Alexander's partner.

Also in 1851 Jose Diego Sepulveda returned to San Pedro. Years before he had traded his one-fifth interest in Rancho de los Palos Verdes for an interest in Rancho San Bernardino and went there to live. Juan and Jose welcomed their brother back and gave him permission to graze his cattle. Diego's interest extended beyond ranching and he soon began hauling passengers from Sepulveda Landing to Los Angeles.

Juan and Jose sold Sepulveda Landing in 1852 to Augustus W. Timms, who had come to San Pedro in the late 1840s. Starting a commission and freighting business in competition with Alexander, Timms improved the wharf and built a corral, warehouse and other structures at the landing. In time, this area came to be called Timms Point.*

*California Historical Landmark No. 384 and Los Angeles City Historic-Cultural Monument No. 171.

The competition that grew between Timms and Banning became legend. The two often drove their own stagecoaches and raced each other to Los Angeles at breakneck speeds over roads that were described as abominably bad. Business in Southern California boomed, partly because of the discovery of small deposits of gold in the local mountains and foothills in 1853. As many as six stage-coach and freighting companies competed on the Harbor-to-Los Angeles route, driving passenger fares down from ten dollars to fifty cents. That summer, Banning and Alexander gained an advantage over their competitors when they brought in four Concord coaches from the East and put them into service.

For much of the way through San Pedro, the road to Los Angeles followed the route of today's Gaffey Street. Near its present intersection with Channel Street, Diego Sepulveda built what is believed to have been the first two-story, Monterey-type adobe* in Southern California. With its upper veranda and two immense pepper trees in front, the house became a landmark to all entering or leaving San Pedro.

Also in 1853 San Pedro was designated a Port of Entry with its own custom house. The Pacific Mail Steamship Company included San Pedro as a regular port of call on its San Francisco–Mazatlan run, but as San Pedro was considered an inconsequential port, the service was somewhat erratic. In 1854 Banning along with Benjamin D. Wilson, John G. Downey and William Sanford purchased 2,400 acres at less than one dollar an acre from Manuel Dominguez, who was facing legal expenses in protecting his title to Rancho San Pedro. The low-lying acreage bordered the shallow inner bay that lay protected by a long, curving spit of land called *Isla de la Culebra de Cascabel* ("Rattlesnake Island").** That acreage eventually became the community of Wilmington, but at the time of purchase, knowing men called it "Banning's Folly," "Banning's goose pond" and other derisive names.

There seems to be no documentation to show precisely whether there was a clearly defined community at San Pedro in the first twenty years after the American takeover. The Port of San Pedro was apparently comprised of the few commercial structures that were erected in the area of the old Hide House and at Timms Point. What kind of a community may have existed here can only be surmised. The following extract from the May 16, 1857, edition of the *Los Angeles Star* tells us: "San Pedro is not a place of much pretension in the way of houses, but the few there are occupied in

*The site of this adobe is designated California Historical Landmark No. 380.
**The nucleus of today's highly developed Terminal Island.

View of Sepulveda rancho reproduced by permission of The Huntington Library, San Marino, Calif.

the most profitable manner. At the landing of Banning & Wilson there is an extensive blacksmith shop, also a carriage manufactory, a saddlery and harness-making establishment, where the wagons, etc., required in their extensive transportation business are manufactured and repaired. There are also extensive warehouses, stables, corrals, etc. Also a grocery, provision and liquor store and hotel.

"The Custom-house is at this landing, the duties of which for a long time have been discharged by Deputy Collector J.F. Stevens. For the accommodation of the public a wharf has been erected on the beach, at which boats receive and land passengers and freight. A short distance from this point is Timms' landing. A pier of considerable extent has been erected for the shipment of merchandise; ample storage is provided in an immense warehouse;

Turn-of-the-century view of the Don Jose Diego Sepulveda home built in 1853. Regarded as the first two-story, Monterey-type adobe in Southern California, it stood near the northwest corner of Channel and Gaffey Streets and was razed before 1910.

Inset (top): The overall view shows the rancho to the southeast. The bluff at left overlooks the present-day Todd Shipyard.

Inset (bottom): **DECEMBER 1900.** *According to notes on the original photograph, these people were guests at a "Diego feed" (Sunday barbecue) at the Sepulveda hacienda.*

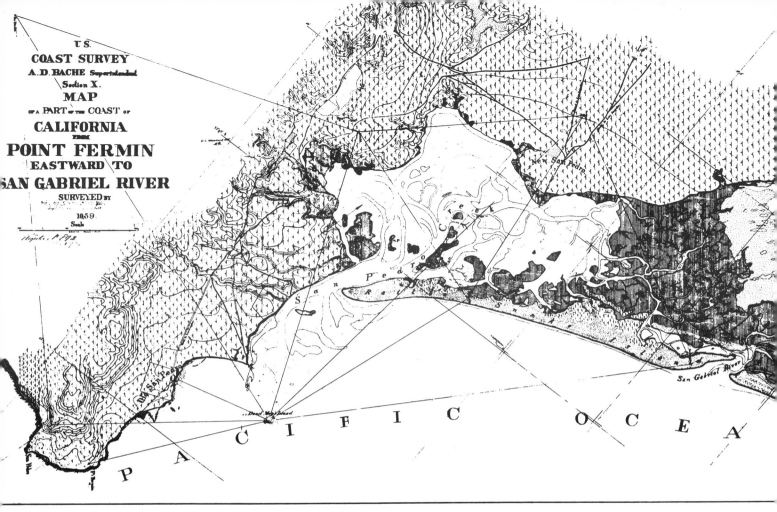

1859. *For more than 300 years, sea captains found the Port of San Pedro basically as it appears in this coastal survey drawing. Casa de San Pedro and the original port were in the cove curving north and east from the square marked Old San Pedro seen at lower left. Wilmington grew on the site marked New San Pedro at right of center. An early outlet of the San Gabriel River is seen at the right. The present mouth of the river was stabilized east of Long Beach near Alamitos Bay. It appears the surveyors transposed the designations of Points Fermin and San Pedro at far left.*

barges and boats of all kinds for the conveyance of goods and passengers to and from the steamers and sailing crafts, are also on hand."*

In the fall of 1858 Banning completed his wharf in the inner bay and transferred his operations there. His facilities were now sheltered from the forces of the open sea and, in addition, he was over six miles closer to Los Angeles on the overland haul. A small community called New San Pedro, or sometimes San Pedro New Town, began its development there. A hydrographic survey of the inner bay was completed in 1859. The resulting chart shows a string of about thirty-five structures of all kinds along the entire stretch of shore from New San Pedro to the old Hide House, a distance of approximately seven miles.

When the Civil War broke out, Banning and Benjamin D. Wilson, one of his partners, deeded sixty acres to the government for a consideration of one dollar and Camp Drum was established. During the war thousands of Union troops were stationed at the camp, which was renamed Drum Barracks.** New San Pedro thrived

*As quoted in Thompson and West, *History of Los Angeles County, California*, p. 144.

**California Historical Landmark No. 169 and Los Angeles City Historic-Cultural Monument No. 21.

and Banning's business boomed as he hauled military supplies throughout the Southwest and sold provisions to the army. He was commissioned a brigadier general in the California Militia by Governor John G. Downey.

New San Pedro's name was changed to Wilmington in 1863 and a post office was established there the following year. Banning, who had been living in a house on Canal Street (now Avalon Boulevard) since moving to the Inner Harbor, completed building a mansion* in 1865. It was probably the most luxurious home in Southern California at that time.

The army abandoned Drum Barracks in 1866, but the community of Wilmington was well established by then, having attracted the bulk of the shipping business from San Pedro. The Los Angeles and San Pedro Railroad, with its terminus at Banning's wharf in Wilmington, was built in 1869. Harbor development projects were begun shortly thereafter. The 1870 census recorded a population of 942 for Wilmington, as the whole of the harbor area had come to be known. The official census tabulations compare this with a population of 359 for 1860, when the area was known as San Pedro. The tabulation is footnoted that San Pedro was abolished and all 1870 population statistics for the harbor area are shown under Wilmington.

The government sold the Drum Barracks' buildings at public auction in 1877. Benjamin Wilson purchased and donated some of them to the Methodist Episcopal Church South, which opened a college there. The school was named Wilson College in his honor, and though operated barely fifteen years, it was a forerunner of the private colleges founded in Southern California during the boom period of the eighties.

Shipping activities continued to be conducted in the same manner as in Spanish and Mexican days. Large ships anchored in the exposed roadstead of the bay and unloaded cargo to barges and ships' boats for transfer to shore, a method known as *lighterage*. If San Pedro were to achieve significance as a port, deep-water facilities protected from the forces of winds and waves would have to be constructed, thereby enabling large vessels to unload directly to the shore and eliminating the use of lighters. Phineas Banning and his associates recognized this need and thought the answer was in developing the Inner San Pedro Bay, called San Pedro Slough and later Wilmington Slough. It was sheltered by Rattlesnake Island that extended west and south from the mainland, near

Courtesy, Banning Residence Museum.

PHINEAS BANNING

Phineas Banning arrived in San Pedro in 1851 and quickly rose to managing the port warehouse and running fast stages to the pueblo. In 1858 he founded Wilmington and began a harbor. He brought the railroad, telegraph and U.S. Army to the community and acquired the rank of general in the California State Militia. Banning is popularly credited as being the "Father of the Harbor."

*California Historical Landmark No. 147 and Los Angeles City Historic-Cultural Monument No. 25.

where the Henry Ford Bridge now stands, to a point across the main ship channel approximately opposite the foot of Sixth Street. About a mile farther south was Deadman's Island, a rocky promontory some fifty feet high and two–and–one-half acres at its base, that stood inside of where Reservation Point on Terminal Island is today. When Deadman's Island was removed to widen the Main Channel in the 1920s, the material was used as fill to create that part of Terminal Island.

Sandbars running from Deadman's to Rattlesnake Island and to the mainland prevented all but very shallow-draught vessels from entering this sheltered lagoon, which was roughly three miles long and 2,000 yards at its widest point. The water averaged only a few feet deep at high tide and in most of the lagoon the bottom mud lay exposed when the tide ebbed. Myriad channels, some reaching a depth of twenty feet, snaked through the mudflats. Banning staked his money that these channels were navigable and built a 700-foot wharf on the acreage purchased from Manuel Dominguez in 1854. The wharf extended out to one of the deeper channels.

On October 1, 1858, Banning's steam tug, *Medora*, towed cargo-laden lighters to his new landing — an event that marked the first development in the Inner Harbor. In 1861 the coasting schooner *Lewis Perry*, drawing eleven feet, became the first seagoing vessel to be towed across the bar. It was also the first oceangoing ship to unload in the harbor directly to a wharf without the assistance of lighters. This occasion moved an unidentified scribe to write: "We expect to see coasting steamers making their regular trips to New Town [Wilmington] discharging freight and loading passengers on the wharf, safe from the dangers of rough weather, instead of lying off to sea, subjecting life and property to the perils of southeast gales and the breakers . . . . It will happen yet!"*

Removing the sandbars that restricted entry into the inner bay and dredging channels that could be negotiated by deep-draught ships were prime requirements for the creation of an adequate

CIRCA 1880. *Timms Point and Landing by this date included a hotel, which was intended for passengers in transit but later became popular with summer vacationists. Today the site is submerged about 100 yards from the inner end of the Fishermen's Slip near Ports O'Call. Timms and Phineas Banning competed in the freight and passenger business to and from the Pueblo de Los Angeles.* (See inside front cover, no. 4.)

*As quoted in Harris Newmark, *Sixty Years in Southern California, 1853-1913*, p. 290. The wharf described was located at what is now the foot of Avalon Boulevard.

port. U.S. Army engineers confirmed that by building a break-water between the tip of Rattlesnake Island and Deadman's Island, the tidal flow would be constricted and a current of sufficient force created to clear away the sandbar and deepen the channel. Lobbying in Congress resulted in $200,000 in federal funds for harbor improvements and work on the breakwater began in 1871. After nine years and a total expenditure of $480,000, a 4,700-foot bulk-head of heavy timbers and a 2,000-foot stone jetty closed the gap between Rattlesnake and Deadman's. On the ocean side, waves deposited silt against the breakwater and the southern portions of today's Terminal Island began to take shape. A jetty extending east and south from Timms Point acted as a training wall that guided the current which kept the channel entrance clear of silt deposits.

As many as 600 men working with the aid of seven steam–powered pile drivers were employed on the project at one time. Upon completion the depth at the entrance to the inner bay ranged from eleven feet at mean low water to seventeen feet during the spring tides. Shallow-draught steamers and schooners regularly entered the inner harbor to tie up directly to Banning's wharf to discharge and take on cargo. Larger vessels, however, were still obliged to anchor in the outer bay and discharge to lighters. Much remained to be done before San Pedro — known officially as the Port of Wilmington since 1874 — would become a deep-water port.

The Point Fermin Lighthouse* was built in 1874. Miss Mary L. Smith was appointed the first lighthousekeeper and she lived there with her sister, Helen. However, they soon left the light-house because of loneliness, the nearest town being Wilmington. As breakwater construction and dredging operations continued, more people came to the harbor. From the construction camps set up on Rattlesnake Island grew the original community of East San Pedro. On the mainland side, the seeds of a community took root as families moved in to create tiny settlements north of Timms Landing.

While harbor improvements progressed, efforts were being made to link Los Angeles with the transcontinental rail system. By offering all the stock in the Los Angeles and San Pedro Railroad and a cash subsidy of $377,000, Los Angeles convinced the Southern Pacific Railroad to lay its track through the city when it constructed the line from San Francisco to El Paso, Texas. The Southern Pacific completed the line to Los Angeles in 1876 and the Port of Wilmington was linked to the transcontinental system.

*National Register of Historic Places.

The 1880 census counted 911 people in Wilmington, including the areas of San Pedro and Rattlesnake Island. In 1881 the Southern Pacific extended its track across the inner bay, then called Wilmington Lagoon, and brought the railroad to San Pedro, establishing its terminal at the base of the bluff below present-day Tenth Street. In the process the railroad acquired title to the land fronting the channel all the way to Timms Point. On August 16, 1882, the first through-passenger train from Los Angeles arrived at San Pedro and the community began the steady growth that continues to this day. In 1883 San Pedro was large enough to warrant a post office of its own. The boom of the eighties had reached the community but it was not to be all fair winds and clear sailing. San Pedro was firmly in the grip of the "Octopus," as the Southern Pacific Railroad was called.

During the thirty years of commercial growth following the American takeover, the rancheros, hard hit by a series of economic and natural calamities, did not share in the general prosperity. The quick riches of the gold rush vanished when cattle driven from Missouri, Texas and Mexico glutted the market and knocked down the price of beef. Then came three years of drought and cattle starved when the hot sun parched the grazing lands. The tax list of 1864 showed most ranches with liens against them for delinquent taxes.

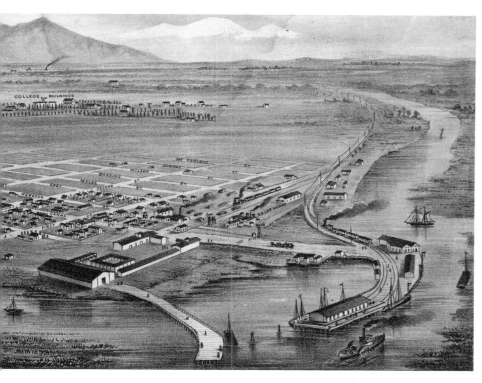

For Juan and Jose Sepulveda legal actions complicated matters. As the grant was in their names, they bore the expense of defending their title in court. Pressed for cash, Juan mortgaged his one-fifth interest in 1856 for $5,000. The next year his brother, Diego, bought the interest for $3,000 at a mortgage foreclosure sale. Other interests were sold over succeeding years and a tangle of litigation developed as a series of partition suits were filed. Diego Sepulveda died in 1869 and his children fought hard to preserve their inherited interest in the land. In the midst of this litigation, Juan and Jose finally received the patent giving them clear title in 1880. But by that time it meant little. In September, 1882, a final court decree partitioned Rancho de los Palos Verdes. Most of the peninsula went to Jotham Bixby in the 17,000 acres awarded to him. Augustus Timms received 700 acres on Point Fermin and about 650 acres were reserved for the as yet unincorporated Town of San Pedro. By today's landmarks the original boundaries of the town were Santa Cruz Street on the north, Pacific Avenue on the west, Fort MacArthur on the south and the harbor channel on the east. The children of Diego Sepulveda (Aurelio, Roman and Rudecinda) salvaged 4,000 acres west of Pacific Avenue between Capitol Drive and the ocean while Juan Sepulveda himself was left with 12.47 acres. For his brother the legal battles and disappointments were over: Jose had died in February, 1881.

1877. *Resurging after a post–Civil War slump, Wilmington as illustrated here had an impressive waterfront: wharves, a large warehouse and direct ship-to-rail connections. Square-block estates are seen west of "downtown" and numerous windmills attest to a fresh water table beneath. The Los Angeles River, following the course of what became Dominguez Slough after 1920, is discreetly shaded in on the east side of town. Phineas Banning's residence at upper center adjoins the Drum Barracks that by this time had become Wilson College.*

3

SAN PEDRO'S GOLDEN AGE

THE DECADE OF THE EIGHTIES dawned on a San Pedro that was little more than a few frame houses and shacks scattered along the channel shore. The workmen brought in during the seventies to build the breakwater had been lodged in camps on Rattlesnake Island and some of them had found their way to San Pedro. By this time the embarcadero and the area around the Hide House were known as Old San Pedro. The bulk of shipping activity had moved north to Timms Point and up the inner bay to Wilmington. The point had grown into a modest complex of warehouses, hotel and a store. It was a favorite beach resort for people from Los Angeles. A little distance north, families had gathered in small settlements. In his book Harris Newmark described it succinctly: "In the late seventies, a Portuguese named Fayal settled near what is now the corner of Sixth and Front streets, San Pedro; and one Lindskow took up his abode in another shack a block away. Around these rude huts sprang up the neighborhoods of Fayal and Lindville, since absorbed by San Pedro."* Named after Martin E. Lindskow, a lighterman originally from Denmark, Lindville grew to seven families. Fayal's proper name was Manuel Duarte. He was reputed to have come from the island of Fayal in the Azores.

*Harris Newmark, *Sixty Years in Southern California, 1853-1913*, pp. 404-5.

Opposite page: CIRCA 1900. *Plaza Park, looking north toward Wilmington, is the setting for this photo of Mr. and Mrs. Muret Phillips and daughter Marvel posing in their finery. The photo was probably taken by Mrs. Phillips' brother Ernest Wood, an early San Pedro photographer.*

1878. *This original drawing of Lindskow Landing, located at the foot of Fifth and Front Streets just north of Stingaree Gulch, shows "Lindville" and the homes of Martin E. Lindskow, William Crittenden and Henry Crocker. The artist is T.F. Keaveny.*

LATE 1880s. *Front Street (now Harbor Boulevard) looking south from Nob Hill at Fourth Street. A devastating fire in 1891 wiped out the block between Fifth and Sixth Streets; thereafter, brick construction became mandatory.*

By contrast, Wilmington had been laid out as a town site when founded in 1858 as New San Pedro. It was incorporated in 1872 and in 1880 boasted Wilson College, established six years earlier to provide students with "a thorough classical and practical education. It has every advantage of healthful climate, ease of access, freedom from those temptations so ruinous to the young, pleasant surroundings, etc., etc."* There was also a grade school built in 1863 with two teachers and 110 students. Two churches served the religious needs of the community. These were Saints Peter and Paul (originally called "Saint Peter"), a Catholic church built in 1865 with the aid of soldiers from Drum Barracks (who donated their labor), and the Cavalry Presbyterian Church** built in 1870: The latter structure stands today on Marine Avenue, after having been moved twice in its 110-year existence. From 1876 Episcopal services were held in the basement of the Banning Mansion until 1883, when Saint John's Episcopal Church☆ was built. Much of the cost of materials was donated by the Bannings. Wilmington also boasted lodges for four fraternal orders and a thirty-five–member volunteer fire department to protect life and property.

All through the seventies Jotham Bixby, a prosperous rancher, had been acquiring interests in Rancho de los Palos Verdes. Along with other interest holders, he laid out the streets and tracts of

*Thompson and West, *History of Los Angeles County, California*, p. 145.

**Los Angeles City Historic-Cultural Monument No. 155.

☆Los Angeles City Historic-Cultural Monument No. 47.

the San Pedro town site on the channel shore. They found ready buyers for their lots among seamen, railroaders and people involved in the breakwater construction. Shipping activity and port development projects were increasing. A wharf constructed at Timms Point allowed large steamers to discharge just inside the bar. To the north the Pacific Coast Steamship Company built a 1,200-foot wharf. When Southern Pacific extended its track into San Pedro, the stage was set for the community to bloom.

All this development made it imperative that the various interests in the Sepulveda land grant be made clear and this could only be achieved through partition of the property. A series of interlocutory decrees issued through the years to May, 1881, culminated in the final decree of partition issued in September, 1882. In addition to distributing the rancho's vast acreage to the plaintiffs, the decree designated ownership of town lots that were shown on a plat prepared by Charles T. Healey. He had been commissioned by Jotham Bixby, who was making the largest claim against the Sepulvedas. Streets and alleys, public school lots and the Plaza on Beacon Street overlooking the channel were all confirmed as surveyed and entered on the Healey plat. This plat became the first official map of the City of San Pedro.

The population explosion in Southern California in the eighties and the extension of the railroads throughout the Southwest increased the importance of the harbor at San Pedro. Here was an economic base on which the new town could grow. By 1883 San Pedro had a school and also a newspaper — the *Shipping Gazette,* with Captain J. F. Janes, editor. The two-story Crocker's Hall was built that year as a public meeting place. It became home for fraternal orders and religious groups that were without their own places of worship. The community's first church, Saint Peter's Episcopal Church,* was built in 1884. This building still stands

*Los Angeles City Historic-Cultural Monument No. 53.

CIRCA 1899. *The ruins of the Hide House, Casa de San Pedro, stood on the Military Reserve (Fort MacArthur). Nothing now remains of the adobe structure built by the trading firm of Hartnell and McCulloch.*

and is now maintained in Harbor View Memorial Park, San Pedro's first cemetery. In 1888 Augustus W. Timms donated the three acre parcel to the township; the land was already being used as a burial ground. Saint Andrew's Presbyterian Church was constructed in that same year. Also in 1888 the first Methodist Episcopal Church was organized but did not erect its own place of worship until 1891, when material salvaged from the wreckage and cargo of the lumber schooner *San Luis* was used in its construction. The Roman Catholics built the first Mary Star of the Sea Church in 1889.

It was during this decade that many of the town fathers came to San Pedro. The names of some have been commemorated through their being used to identify streets and public places in the community. Others are remembered through businesses that they started which still survive, and in many cases bear their names. Many of their descendants live in the community today.

After many visits as a conductor on the Southern Pacific, George H. Peck settled in San Pedro in 1886 and became a successful real estate developer, contractor and banker. The stately mansion that he constructed on Signal Street overlooking Timms Point still stands, though on another site (380 West Fifteenth Street), in a much altered condition. Aurelio Sepulveda, his brother, Roman, and sister, Rudecinda, were among the town's original subdividers. Aurelio built an imposing home near Peck's, while Roman had his residence erected in 1883 on Fifth near West Street. Rudecinda lived with her husband, James H. Dodson, a merchant and municipal officer, in a mansion on the corner of Seventh and Beacon Streets. The Dodson House* survives today at 859 West Thirteenth Street.

*Los Angeles City Historic-Cultural Monument No. 147.

1905. *George Peck is appropriately pictured on a teeter-totter with his daughters. His philanthropies provided the bulk of local park sites and recreational facilities. Alma, Rena, Leland and Peck Parks are among his best known gifts. Peck subdivided many tracts of land in San Pedro and organized the original Bank of San Pedro (1889). He also paid for the laying of the Pacific Electric tracks from downtown to Point Fermin.*

GEORGE H. PECK

JAMES H. DODSON, SR.

RUDECINDA FLORENCIA
SEPULVEDA DE DODSON

CIRCA 1889. *This waterfront scene was photographed from across the channel looking west. The cupola of the Clarence Hotel is seen on the bluff in center. The glassy water reflects two rivals: a three-mast schooner and the more efficient though less majestic steam schooner* NEWSBOY.

1881. *James H. Dodson, Sr., is seen at the time of his marriage to Rudecinda Sepulveda. Born on Rancho San Pedro in 1861, he was twice mayor of San Pedro and postmaster for many years. Dodson Avenue is named for this early leader.*

1881. *Rudecinda Florencia Sepulveda is pictured at the time of her marriage to James H. Dodson. Long San Pedro's reigning grand dame, she donated several plots of property for public use including Plaza Park and the Woman's Clubhouse (formerly at the corner of Eleventh and Gaffey Streets).*

The James H. and Rudecinda Sepulveda Dodson home was built on the southwest corner of Seventh and Beacon Streets, circa 1886. This photo shows the house as it appeared about the turn of the century.

The Edouard Amar House (1888) stood at the corner of Twelfth and Mesa Streets. Razed in the early 1970s, it was replaced by condominiums, but the two palm trees still stand. Members of the Amar family standing in front are Eloi, Edouard, Josephine, Leon and Irma.

Edouard Amar, pioneer sheep rancher, herded his flocks over the San Pedro Hills and close to town in the last decades of the nineteenth century. Sometimes sheep strayed into the yards of residences, schools and the downtown business area.

John N. Malgren, who had been working as a longshoreman for the Southern Pacific since 1875, received the first property deed in the unincorporated town in 1882 in an area called Nob Hill. John Swinford arrived in 1882 and founded the San Pedro Building Supply Company. He built the public meeting hall that bore his name. Anthony and Frank DiRocco, natives of Italy, arrived in 1883 and were pioneers in the fishing industry here. Their descendants have been active in harbor, mercantile and civic affairs of the community to the present day. William G. Kerckhoff was a lumber

CIRCA 1890s. *The original Fifth Street School (1885) was located between Fifth and Sixth Streets where the San Pedro County Courts Building now stands. This view shows the east wing facing Centre Street. (See inside front cover, no. 16.)*

WILLIAM H. SAVAGE

William H. Savage served as state senator for eight years and was quite vocal in his opposition to consolidation of the Harbor Area and Los Angeles. He practiced law, presided as a justice of the peace and was elected city attorney, assemblyman and state senator.

dealer and banker. Albert G. Barton served as an early postmaster. William H. Savage was an attorney, judge, state senator and one of the organizers of the volunteer fire department in 1889. From 1875 French-born Edouard Amar had been raising sheep in the hills along where Gaffey Street now runs. The distinctive Amar home, built about 1888, stood at Twelfth and Mesa Streets until it fell victim to a bulldozer in the early 1970s. This is only a random sampling of founding fathers; there are many others equally deserving of mention who have been omitted here.

The early settlers of San Pedro tended to group themselves into little villages and neighborhoods. Radiating around the business district, which spread along Front (now Harbor Boulevard) and Beacon Streets across the mouth of Stingaree Gulch, between Fourth and Seventh Streets, these areas took on their own identities. South of the business district and rising above the gulch was Vinegar (or South) Hill, one of the "better" neighborhoods.

1895. *At a gathering of the French Colony, Edouard Amar is seen in his shirt sleeves standing at the left corner of the double window on the right.*

A turn-of-the-century view of Front Street (later renamed Harbor Boulevard) is seen from Nob Hill looking south from Fourth Street. In 1928 the boulevard was extended and cut through the eastern side of Plaza Park, reducing it to half the original width. Prominent in the foreground is the windmill that pumped water for the adjacent tank. The Southern Pacific railway station is nearby. The steeple of the First Presbyterian Church is seen at far right. (See inside front cover, no. 12.)

North of the gulch was Nob Hill with its elegant homes, while Barton Hill rose beyond to the north and west. Between these two heights of respectability nestled Happy (or Paradise) Valley, notorious for its saloons and houses of ill-repute. The January 5, 1883, edition of the *Shipping Gazette* reported that a village called "New Jerusalem" had been laid out and one house built. The following January the paper reported that six houses were built at "New Sweden," as the east side of West Street (now Pacific Avenue) between Fourth and Seventh Streets was called.

Before the decade was over there were in San Pedro, in addition to the churches: a public school, four meeting halls, seven hotels (plus one out in the country at Point Fermin), a bank, two commercial buildings, an electric power plant, a public library, a drug store, two markets, a hospital, two newspapers — the *Harbor Advocate* and the *Times* (the *Shipping Gazette* had folded in December, 1884), a volunteer fire department, a literary society and a welfare society. This was the community which blossomed from the few rude shacks that greeted the decade. San Pedro was incorporated as a city of the sixth class on March 1, 1888.

EARLY 1900s. *This postcard scene shows the Presbyterian Church located at Tenth and Mesa Streets. The church tower has since been removed and other cosmetic changes have occurred. The building is now occupied by the Congregation of the Apostolic Assembly of the Faith in Christ Jesus.*

Presbyterian Church, San Pedro, California

EARLY 1900s. *Looking north from Seventh and Beacon Streets, this scene shows the building (left foreground) from which land developer George H. Peck conducted his extensive realty business. Upon his death in 1940, a large trust fund was established to develop and maintain numerous parks and playground facilities in San Pedro. One of the most recent uses of Peck funds was for the Memorial Center in Peck Park.*

Peniel Mission was one of the earliest evangelistic efforts to offset sin in San Pedro. The building stood at the base of Nob Hill facing south at Fourth and Front Streets.

CIRCA 1900. *This popular view of the Main Channel Inner Harbor shows one of Kerckhoff-Cuzner's three identical schooners being escorted to their lumber wharf near Boschke Slough by Banning Co.'s tug-passenger steamer WARRIOR. Across the channel East San Pedro is still a mere strip of sand bolstered by the jetty completed in 1874. One of the Pacific Coast Steamship Co.'s early wooden passenger boats lies alongside the depot. The first local cannery, California Fish Company, occupies the inner end of the pier. The summer colony at Brighton Beach is visible behind the four-mast schooner.*

The exploding population of Los Angeles and environs created an insatiable demand for goods of all kinds, especially lumber. The channel was deepened to eighteen feet in 1888 and that year 500,000 tons of cargo moved through the port. Southern Pacific improved its wharf complex and port activities continued to shift from Wilmington to the deeper water of the channel and Timms Point. Los Angeles had become more dependent than ever on the Port of San Pedro. The Southern Pacific Railroad controlled the harbor frontage as well as the rail and freight rates to the growing city.

The informality with which business had been conducted in the early days was not acceptable to the Southern Pacific. With its monopolistic control of the harbor in place since the late 1870s, the "Octopus" imposed its will. Freight rates, demurrage and schedules were dictated by the railroad and all attempted competition was effectively crushed. In 1885 another railroad giant appeared

CIRCA 1900. *Mitchell Duffy, who came to San Pedro in 1882, established the first regular cross–channel ferry service to East San Pedro on Rattlesnake Island, renamed Terminal in 1890. Rowboats used at the start gave way to gasoline launches, the first of which is shown here at Fifth Street Landing. Duffy expanded his fleet as needed and built at least six boats for ferry and excursion work over a period of some thirty years. The trunk on the landing float is either from, or destined for, some ship or train across the channel.*

CIRCA 1900s. *Boschke Slough and San Pedro Lumber Company occupied the site of today's Eagle Marine Container Terminal.*

on the scene when the Santa Fe Railroad pushed into Southern California. Unable to acquire water frontage here, Santa Fe ran its track to Redondo Beach, where it constructed a pier in 1888, and established that beach city as a port. In 1891 the Los Angeles Terminal Railway succeeded in laying a track from Los Angeles to Rattlesnake Island, which it had earlier purchased and renamed Terminal Island. The railway built its wharf directly across the channel from that of the Southern Pacific.

An early-in-the-century view shows Halfway House, which stood at the foot of Goat Hill (presently Knoll Hill). The restaurant facing north on Front Street (Harbor Boulevard) was operated by the Pauluzzi family and was a popular stop for food and refreshments. Gerardo and Aurelio Pauluzzi ("Big" and "Little Choppo") are the two little boys behind the horse.

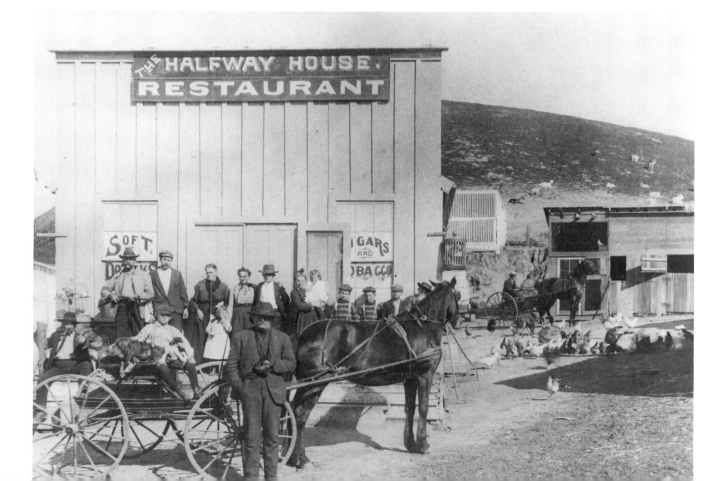

44

The Bethel Ship, a seamen's hostel and mission in East San Pedro, was located behind the Salt Lake Wharf. It was built over the condemned hull of Banning's tug-passenger boat WARRIOR *by Captain Charles Farr in 1902.*

Captain Farr is seated in his office at the rear of the meeting hall. Unused for several years, the mission ship was burned to expedite channel widening operations.

From Laurance L. Hill, *La Reina* (Los Angeles: Security Trust and Savings Bank, 1929).

STEPHEN M. WHITE

Stephen M. White is honored and remembered for his valiant battle in the United States Senate to establish a deep seaport at San Pedro. His three-day debate with Senator William P. Frye of Maine, who favored Santa Monica for the harbor site, was one of the most sensational in Senate history.

Sixteenth Street School was built at Sixteenth and Mesa Streets about 1901 at a cost of $25,000. After the annexation of San Pedro to Los Angeles, the name was changed to Fifteenth Street School to avoid a duplication of names in the Los Angeles District. High school students attended classes here until the high school was completed in 1906. This building burned down in 1922 and was replaced by the present structure.

The new railroads broke Southern Pacific's monopoly. Under the leadership of Collis P. Huntington, the Southern Pacific began to develop a harbor at Santa Monica, where it had complete control of the shoreline. A 4,720-foot pier was constructed to reach the deep water of the bay and by 1893 Santa Monica was attracting a good deal of shipping away from San Pedro. In addition, Huntington was exerting his vast influence on the United States Congress to make Santa Monica the beneficiary of some $3 million to be appropriated for developing a deep-water harbor to serve Los Angeles. Though two boards of engineers had recommended San Pedro as the best candidate for port development, Huntington's influence was such that in 1896 the Senate Committee on Commerce selected Santa Monica. Fortunately, San Pedro was the choice of California's Senator Stephen M. White and he was successful in tying the appropriation to the recommendation of a new board of engineers. In 1897 Rear Admiral John G. Walker submitted the board's report selecting San Pedro and the controversy over where to locate the harbor was finally settled.

The keys to harbor development were construction of a breakwater to provide a protected anchorage and dredging of the Inner Harbor to permit entry of deep-draught vessels. The biggest celebration in San Pedro's history took place on April 26, 1899, when the first barge-load of rock was dumped to begin the 9,250-foot segment of the breakwater extending generally eastward starting about 1,800 feet off San Pedro Point. It was estimated that between 10,000 and 15,000 people gathered at the point to witness the event, partake of a barbecue lunch and serve as willing targets of the horde of real estate men who had arranged the whole celebration. *(Continued on p. 55)*

1899. Visitors are viewing the harbor scene from Plaza Park during the Jubilee celebrating the start of the Federal Breakwater construction. The Southern Pacific Railroad wharf, seen below the bluff, occupied the frontage between Fifth and Ninth Streets. Open water between the wharf and the shore offered sheltered tieup for such small craft as were able to pass between the pier pilings.

Following pages: The Federal Breakwater project is observed here in full swing as the double trainload of granite is pushed up Plaza Park grade by two locomotives under full heads of steam. The gentleman in white shirt and dark tie on the front flatcar indicates a special occasion. Note the strings of rock-laden cars beneath the pedestrian bridge at Tenth Street waiting to be hauled. The walkway provided a safe and convenient access to the wharf and the early railway depot. Two passenger coaches are visible at the far right while a row of sailing lumber schooners imply that business is thriving at the moment.

The configuration of the two-mile *Federal Breakwater (extending eastward from the present Cabrillo Beach) was marked by this trestle from which rock was dumped from railway flatcars. The project, begun in 1899 and completed in 1912, required three million tons of rough granite and squared cap rocks. It represented the efforts of two contracting firms and the U.S. Army Corps of Engineers. By today's standards, the total cost of $3 million was an incredible bargain.*

Inset: JULY 8, 1902. *The closeup view shows the pile-driving rig that advanced the trestle as the rockwork progressed.*

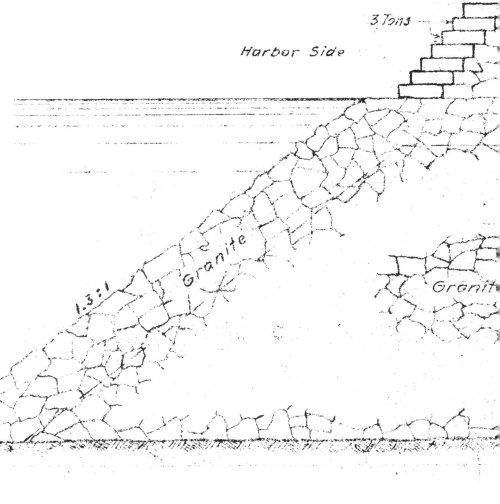

3 Tons

Harbor Side

1.3:1

Granite

Granite

Granit

Another carload of rock is dumped from the trestle as the breakwater is pushed farther out to sea. In total three million tons of granite were placed.

Elev +14.0

8 Tons

Sea Side

El 0.0 Mean Low Water

3:1

El -12.0

Granite

1.2:1

stone

El -52.0

190 Ft. ±

This is a cross section of the breakwater extending from Cabrillo Beach. The broad and relatively rough base was built up to the low-tide line. Then a wall of cut and fitted blocks, reaching a height of fourteen feet, completed the structure. The middle breakwater (1932) was completed without the cap rock as an economy measure.

BREAKWATER

1906. *San Pedro's first high school was located on Gaffey between Twelfth and Thirteenth Streets. Severely damaged by the earthquake of 1933, it was replaced in 1936 by new facilities on Fifteenth Street.*

The City of San Pedro was served by many city halls, of which this is the only one still standing. The structure was built in 1905 for Mayor Edward Mahar on the corner of Eleventh and Palos Verdes Streets. It was used in this capacity until the new domed city hall was completed in 1908. Since then, the building has housed a fire department headquarters (The 1905 volunteer firemen are pictured here), a hotel and a store. In later years the decorative trim was removed.

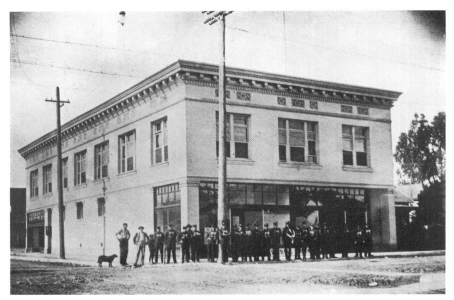

1906. *The headquarters of the South Coast Yacht Club was on the bluff just north of Twenty-second and Mesa Streets and overlooked the cove below Crescent Avenue. This group has occupied various facilities around the harbor since its organization in 1901. It merged with the Los Angeles Motor Boat Club in 1922 to become the Los Angeles Yacht Club, which is still active.*

The ferry launch BLANCHE, built in 1906, is shown leaving Fifth Street Landing for the 500 foot crossing to East San Pedro. The Terminal Island Ferry made a longer run to the landing at Ferry Street, situated just beyond the ships shown at far right. It was a convenient stop for the Brighton Beach colony visitors.

1903. Fir and redwood lumber in random lengths and widths arrived from the northern mills in every type of vessel, as seen in this view toward the east from Nob Hill. The tramp steamer in the foreground is the PLEIADES. Across the channel on the Terminal Island side is the steam schooner SAN PEDRO (1899) at the Salt Lake Wharf at far right. In the immediate foreground are numerous railroad tracks, sinews binding the Port to Los Angeles and the entire Southwest. Preparations for the East San Pedro landfill can be seen in the background.

Peck's Pavilion (1908) was established by George H. Peck at the western extremity of Point Fermin Park to enhance his Ocean View Subdivision. Sunday dances were a feature at this popular entertain-ment center, attractively painted green with white trim and a bright red roof. Later it was used as a boxing arena and a roller rink until demolished, circa 1925. Point Fermin Lighthouse (1874) is on the left.

This view is seen toward the north from the new Carnegie Library in Plaza Park. Note that the Beacon Street grade has been reduced be-tween Seventh and Eighth Streets. Directly above the Park Cafe at left can be seen the belfry of the 1888 Presbyterian Church.

1908. *A lively day on the San Pedro waterfront between First and Sixth Streets is indicated by an interesting mix of sail and steam vessels* *employed in the coastal passenger, freight and lumber trades. The square rigger is probably a foreign ship laden with coal.*

CIRCA 1908. *Al Larson Boat Shop opened for business in 1902 behind the Salt Lake Wharf just north of* *the Bethel Ship. The boat* CAMI-GUIN *is on the marine ways while being overhauled.*

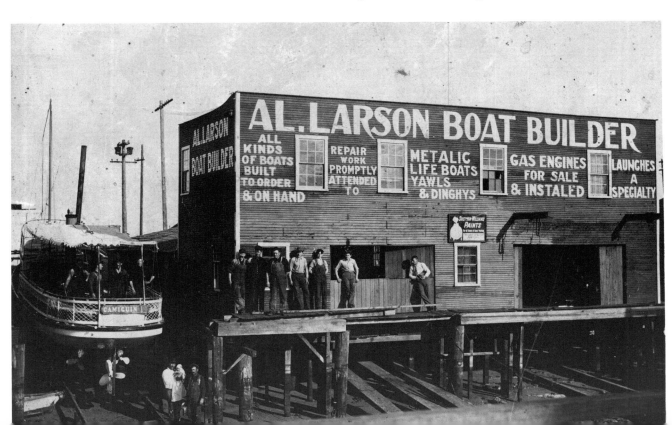

The development brought many new residents to San Pedro. Pacific Electric trolley service was extended to the community in 1904. Dredging and landfill operations began to change the configuration of the waterfront. In 1906 Los Angeles annexed the one-half–to–one–mile–wide, sixteen-mile-long Shoestring Strip that brought its city limit to the Harbor Area. The next year it created the Los Angeles Harbor Commission. A federal Harbor Lines Board laid out the port as it generally appears today and the long-range plan for its development was drawn up. The only obstacle in the path of the proposed development was the absence of

This downtown San Pedro scene toward the northwest is viewed from a ship off the Terminal Island jetty. The domed City Hall at Seventh and Beacon Streets (completed in 1908) is visible to the right of center. The Carnegie Library stands prominently in Plaza Park on Vinegar Hill.

1908. *This waterfront view depicts the Southern Pacific "Steamer Depot" to the left at the foot of Fifth Street, East San Pedro across the channel, Deadman's Island (See inside front cover, no. 24.) in the center background and Front Street curving around the foot of the bluffs. An early-day comfort station stands prominently in the foreground.*

1908. **The visit by President Teddy Roosevelt's Great White Fleet was an occasion for much celebration. This view toward the ferry landing was taken from the intersection of Fifth and Beacon Streets.**

1908. **Civilian visitors and sailors from the Great White Fleet arrived at Fifth Street Landing. Sixteen battleships visited the harbor during a round-the-world good will cruise initiated by President Theodore Roosevelt. This event was probably one of the most dramatic ever experienced here.**

funding. Both San Pedro and Wilmington were too small to provide the tax base needed for the millions of dollars worth of bonds that would have to be floated. Los Angeles was not able to help because it could not legally spend municipal funds on a project outside its boundaries.

Consolidation of the three municipalities seemed to be the answer and with the annexation of the Shoestring Strip the requirement of contiguity had been met. In January, 1909, the California Legislature passed a bill providing for the consolidation of independent cities and each municipality appointed a committee to frame an agreement. Though opposition was vocal and often bitter, when the question was put to the voters of each community in August, 1909, the measure was approved by large majorities, 107 to 61 in Wilmington and 726 to 227 in San Pedro. Los Angeles became a port city and San Pedro and Wilmington, having given up their independence, became districts of the larger city. All were embarked on the twenty-year honeymoon spelled out in the terms of the consolidation agreement.

1908. An anti-consolidation banner is strung across Beacon at Sixth Street. The view is south toward Seventh Street. Local feeling was divided on the prospect of annexation of the little city to Los Angeles, but sentiment finally changed after Wilmington's approval threatened to isolate the port. At center right is Armour's Pharmacy, which became an emergency first aid station when a group of citizens (including Mr. Armour) was assaulted upon returning from a pro-consolidation meeting in Los Angeles. Richard Armour, noted author-humorist, tells this story in Drug- store Days, *wherein his boyhood in San Pedro is recalled. Note the B.P.O.E. (Elks Club) "WEL- COME" sign.*

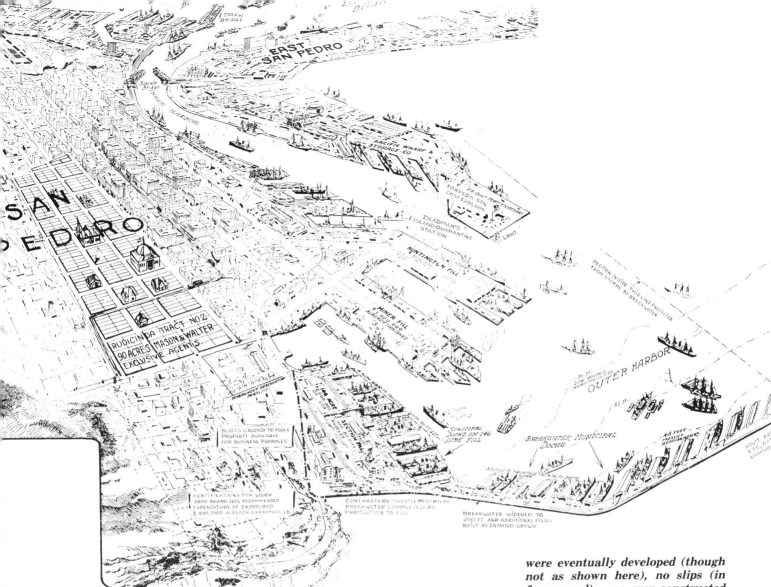

Labels within rendering:

DRAW BRIDGE

EAST SAN PEDRO

SAN PEDRO

Bascule Bridge

INNER HARBOR

PACIFIC WHARF & STORAGE CO.

U.S. GOV'T FORTIFICATIONS

TORPEDO STN. COST $250,000

DEADMAN'S ISLAND QUARANTINE STATION

LIGHT

HUNTINGTON FILL

MINER FILL ALREADY FURNISHED

SECTION INSIDE THIS LINE PROTECTED FROM STORMS BY BREAKWATER

OUTER HARBOR

36 FT. LOW WATER PRESENT MEASUREMENT

42 FT.

RUDICINDA TRACT NO 2
90 ACRES MASON & WALTER
EXCLUSIVE AGENTS.

GOVERNMENT BREAKWATER PIER 3

OUTER HARBOR SECTION FILL

MUNICIPAL DOCKS ON 146 ACRE FILL

BREAKWATER MUNICIPAL DOCKS

4-8 FEET PRESENT MEASUREMENT

BLUFFS GRADED TO MAKE PROPERTY AVAILABLE FOR BUSINESS PURPOSES

FORTIFICATIONS FOR WHICH ARMY BOARD HAS RECOMMENDED EXPENDITURE OF $4,000,000 $400,000 ALREADY APPROPRIATED

CONTRACTORS TRESTLE PORTION OF BREAKWATER COMPLETED AS PROTECTION TO FILL

32,000 FT. FRONTAGE 35 TO 36 FT. DEPTH

BREAKWATER WIDENED TO 200 FT. AND ADDITIONAL PIERS BUILT AS DEMAND GROWS

GOV'T. APP'D. $50,000 LIGHTHOUSE

CIRCA 1909. *This is thought to be a land sales promotion. Box lunches were generally given away at such events. The sign to the far left appears to be that of Bullocks Realty Company.*

1909. *This rendering is from a pro-consolidation article. It depicts Outer Harbor improvements that the promoters claimed would be financed by Los Angeles' immense bonding authority. While the Miner and Huntington Fills at upper left were eventually developed (though not as shown here), no slips (in foreground) were ever constructed along the breakwater. Note that a Bascule Bridge is indicated at approximately where the Vincent Thomas Bridge crosses today. Boschke Slough is retained, thus providing splendid isolation for Smith Island. The misspelling of Rudecinda is obvious.*

The "marriage" of Miss San Pedro and Mr. Los Angeles was performed to symbolize the consolidation of the two cities. Regarded by many as a dubious blessing, the matrimony nonetheless has lasted a full seventy-five years. During this time the romance has mellowed into a comforting partnership wherein neither party can be truly happy without the other. The union has produced a thriving seaport, which now ranks second in the United States and third in the world.

4

THE HONEYMOON

AN PEDRO AND WILMINGTON VOTERS approved consolidation with Los Angeles by a better than three-to-one majority. They traded home rule and control of the harbor for assurances of funding for improvements they could not afford. In addition, the terms of the consolidation agreement promised them municipal services for their fast-growing communities: police and fire protection; branch libraries; market and wharf facilities for the fishing industry; park, sanitation and health services; and a municipally owned and operated ferry service to Terminal Island.

Development of the harbor, however, was the key to the district's future economic well-being, and for this purpose Los Angeles promised to spend $10 million over the next ten years. Much

Gaffey portrait from Security Pacific National Bank Photograph Collection/Los Angeles Public Library.

Opposite page: **JANUARY 3, 1917. This view of Harbor Boulevard Cut (through Nob Hill) looks north from Fourth Street. The equipment used is an interesting mix of old and new paving machinery. Mule teams service a concrete paving machine (right), while steam and motor road rollers are seen on the left. The two mules in the foreground enjoy a brief respite while surveying the scene.**

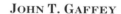

JOHN T. GAFFEY

Inset: **John T. Gaffey, an ardent San Pedro booster, state political leader, real estate developer and financier, married Arcadia Bandini of an old prestigious Californio family.**

The John T. Gaffey House (1905) stood at the southwest corner of Third and Bandini Streets. This carefully planned and landscaped estate later became La Rambla Inn, a restaurant during the 1930s. It was demolished in the early 1960s to make way for the modern YMCA Recreation Center.

Dredging and filling operations extended wharfage into the Outer Harbor below Crescent Avenue and created deep-water berths for large vessels. Shown here is the filling of the 60-acre Huntington Concession, extending approximately three-fourths of a mile south from the Southern Pacific Slip (far right). The work was begun in 1912; when completed in 1914, the mole became Municipal Pier No. 1 on which Warehouse No. 1 was later constructed. Running parallel to the Huntington Concession on its shore side is the 150-acre Miner Fill, completed some years earlier. The white-pillared building in the center background directly below the hilltop is the first San Pedro High School.

San Pedro Transportation Company upgraded the cross-channel ferry service by building the PEER in 1912 for the Terminal Island run and the REAL in 1913 to serve East San Pedro. By 1925 these boats were relegated to standby duty, having been replaced on regular runs by larger craft.

development was already in progress, initiated by private interests after the start of construction of the breakwater. In 1905 John T. Gaffey had organized the Pacific Wharf & Storage Co., which had dredged a turning basin in the Inner Harbor and had begun building a wharf on the Wilmington shore. It then started reclamation and wharf construction operations at the tip of the Terminal Island spit where Southwest Marine, Inc., is today. Just to the north the Los Angeles Terminal Railway was expanding its facilities through an eighty-acre reclamation project. Across the channel at Timms Point, the 1,800-foot Southern Pacific Slip provided dockage for a never-ending stream of lumber vessels. (Today, this is Fishermen's Slip next to Ports O'Call Village and Whalers Wharf.) The mole created by Huntington Fill extended south from the Southern Pacific Slip to reach into the deep water of Outer Harbor. Paralleling it on the west was Miner Fill of Outer Harbor Dock and Wharf Company, in which the Union Oil Company of California had a sizable interest. These fills created acreage that today extends from the base of the bluff below Crescent Avenue and borders East and West Channels and Watchorn Basin.

The petroleum industry had made its entry into the harbor in 1896, when Union Oil constructed a pipeline to East San Pedro to bring crude from the Brea Canyon–Olinda area. For coal-poor California, oil was an important commodity, with three barrels replacing one ton of coal. It had quickly displaced lumber as the leading single commodity handled. In 1904, 13,741 barrels of oil and 500 million board feet of lumber had passed through the harbor. Just two years later petroleum shipments had increased almost eighteen times to 235,159 barrels while lumber had decreased to 447 million board feet. (In fiscal 1980 lumber represented a mere .68 percent of the port's total tonnage, whereas bulk oil, including bunkers, represented 65.58 percent.)

This development had been proceeding in a haphazard manner without an overall plan. Furthermore, private interests were gaining control over the most valuable harbor frontage to the detriment of the "free harbor" concept. Even before consolidation Los Angeles had initiated litigation to test the validity of the titles to much of the shoreline and succeeded in winning a judgment inval-

1914. *This section of the waterfront is the site of the present-day Ports O'Call Village on the Main Channel. The three-story building located on Beacon Street above the bluff was formerly the Victoria Apartments and is now known as Marina View. In the clearing on the right is the 1905, white-brick City Hall on Palos Verdes Street.* (See p. 50.)

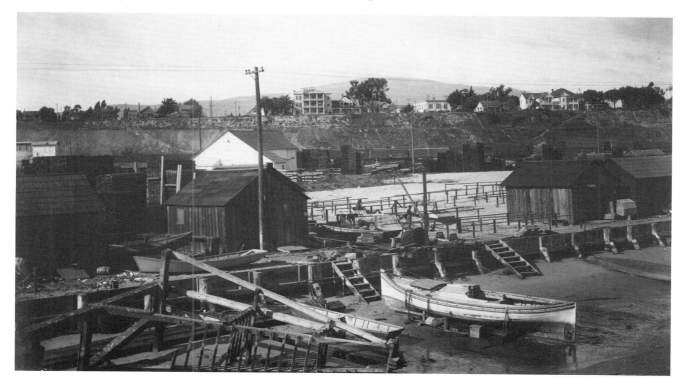

CIRCA 1910. *Four submarines and their tender are docked near Sixth Street during a visit to the port.*

CIRCA 1912. *A variety of seafoods were readily caught in the waters adjacent to the White Point–Portuguese Bend area. This early Japanese farm family has laid out a fresh catch of fish split for drying.*

idating the overwhelming majority of them. In 1911 the California Legislature passed the Los Angeles Tidelands Act, which gave the city control over the harbor. Now the free harbor fight was truly over, although suits contesting the act would drag through the courts until 1920. On adoption of the tidelands act, port facilities became available to all at a fair tariff.

As soon as the consolidation procedure had been completed, Los Angeles floated a $3 million bond issue for harbor improvements. This was the first installment on the promised $10 million. The federal government completed the west arm of the breakwater in 1912, including 1,800 additional feet to close the gap to San Pedro

1911. *San Pedro Hospital, first established in 1906 at Fifth and Palos Verdes Streets, served the community at this site from 1909 to 1917. Completed in 1888 on Nob Hill overlooking Front Street, the building originally housed the elegant Clarence Hotel. The structure was lowered when Nob Hill was cut down to make way for Harbor Boulevard. It became the San Pedro Hotel after World War I.*

Point. The original plans did not call for the breakwater to connect with the shore. In 1913 an additional $2.5 million worth of bonds were issued. In that year also the Port of Los Angeles, as it was now known, became the world's leading lumber port, handling almost one billion board feet. Well over 500,000 tons of other cargo were also handled. San Pedro's population was estimated at over 8,100, far exceeding Wilmington's, which was estimated at 1,800.

As harbor development progressed, so did plans for its defense. An 1888 presidential directive had designated the 500-vara-square Government Reserve of Old San Pedro as a military reservation. In 1906 a Board of Fortifications report estimated the cost

1915. This scene looks northwest at landfill operations in the vicinity of the Smith Island–Boschke Slough area between Harbor Boulevard and the waterfront. It was here that the quaint little village called "Mexican Hollywood" flourished for about 20 years until cleared away in 1950. At upper right a small portion of the Kerckhoff-Cuzner Mill and Lumber Company can be seen.

AUGUST 15, 1916. *Seen at left, looking south on Pacific Avenue from the vicinity of Twenty-sixth Street, is the oldest building at Fort MacArthur, moved in the early 1920s to the east bluff of the fort. The stack of the Trona Kelp Processing Plant (potash) is seen in the background at far left. The original plant building (sans stack) still stands east of Pacific Avenue at about Thirtieth Street. Streetcar tracks ran from downtown to Point Fermin Park.*

of fortifying the port at $2 million and land was subsequently purchased on the slopes of San Pedro Hill behind Point Fermin. In 1914 the post was named Fort MacArthur and a coast artillery battalion took up quarters there. The original Lower Reservation that still stands on the east side of Pacific Avenue between Hamilton Avenue and Twenty-eighth Street is one of only two army posts built in that period to have survived almost intact to this day, though no longer under army jurisdiction.

CIRCA 1916. *White Star Cannery, the original packers of "Chicken of the Sea," was located on the site of the California Fish Company, which had been destroyed by fire. Situated on the Main Channel, the latter was the first cannery in the harbor.*

Municipal Pier No. 1 (Berths 57–60) was completed on the site of Huntington Fill and a Municipal Wholesale Fish Market was established at Berths 79–81. A wooden viaduct was constructed to connect Fourteenth Street on top of the bluff with the wharves at sea level. August, 1914, brought the long-awaited opening of the Panama Canal and the promise of increasing maritime activity. Unfortunately, World War I started in the same month and this had a dampening effect on West Coast trade.

FEBRUARY 3, 1915. *The wooden viaduct leading to Outer Harbor was replaced by the present concrete structure in 1928.*

Harbor development, however, continued. Construction of Warehouse No. 1 on the Municipal Pier was started in 1915 and 100,000 square feet of transit shed were completed at Slip No. 1 in Wilmington. Southwestern Shipbuilding Co. established a shipyard in 1917 on reclaimed acreage on the channel side of Terminal Island. (Bethlehem Steel Corporation later took over the site and Southwest Marine, Inc., occupies it now.) On the east side dredging and wharf construction began for the creation of Fish Harbor. The completion of Fish Harbor attracted canneries to locate there and put the port on a course to becoming the largest fishing industry center in the world. Figures for the fiscal year ending June 30, 1916, showed that over two million tons of cargo of all kinds flowed through the port.

Entry of the United States into the war flooded the shipyards with contracts. Los Angeles Shipbuilding & Drydock Co. (now Todd Shipyards Corporation), Ralph J. Chandler Shipbuilding Co., Fulton Shipbuilding Co. and Southwestern employed more than

1930. *One of the massive fourteen-inch disappearing rifles at Osgood-Farley Battery on the Fort MacArthur Upper Reservation is shown at the moment of firing. The batteries had been constructed between 1914 and 1916 for coastal defense but were obsolete by World War II, and the guns were scrapped thereafter. Battery Osgood-Farley (without the guns) has been placed on the National Register of Historic Places.*

20,000 people to build both steel and wooden vessels, mostly for the war effort. Fort MacArthur became a training center for soldiers destined for France. For protection of the harbor, gun emplacements were built on Deadman's Island to provide support for the huge fourteen-inch guns on the Upper Reservation.

The war period also saw the beginning of the Harbor Area Young Women's Christian Association. Under the auspices of the National YWCA, a few dedicated women served on the War Work Council of San Pedro. They pushed for the opening of a hospitality house as a safe and inexpensive residence for women who were alone. The building,* completed near the end of 1918, is located at 437 West Ninth Street. It was designed by Julia Morgan, the first woman to receive an architectural degree from the Ecole des Beaux Arts in Paris. Later she was the architect of the sumptuous Hearst Castle at San Simeon. A group of interested citizens subsequently purchased the hospitality house and the San Pedro YWCA was organized, receiving its charter in 1921. (In recognition of its growth into a metropolitan-type organization, it officially became the Harbor Area YWCA in 1955.)

With the end of the war in November, 1918, came a boom in home building to house the many people who had flocked to San Pedro. The shipyards were still busy and the resumption of normal maritime activity kept the local economy sound. Tracts were developed west of Meyler Street as well as around Point Fermin, and the city limits were extended uphill as the new areas were

*Los Angeles City Historic-Cultural Monument No. 186.

CIRCA 1920. *Since 1918 the YWCA has provided an invaluable, hospitable environment for San Pedrans. Through the years the programs offered have changed to reflect the needs of the community. As an example, many attendees treasure fond memories of "Playnight," the weekly Friday night dances during the 1940s for eighth and ninth graders of Richard Henry Dana Junior High School.*

EARLY 1920s. *The Alianza Protectora de Obreros pose after participating in a local parade. Lodge No. 1 was founded in San Pedro in 1920 as a protective association of workers. Little is known of this organization although its founding was probably prompted by the labor* struggles of the times. *Composed of "Old Californios" and Hispanic immigrants, the group was unique because of the sentiment prevalent in the community against labor and civil rights organizations. The old Mary Star of the Sea Church is at right background.*

1919. *Looking south from the Five Points area (the junction of Gaffey and Anaheim Streets, Normandie Avenue and Palos Verdes Drive North), North Gaffey Street is shown under construction. This scene il-* lustrates a rather crude but effective road grading process: as the teamster drives forward, excess earth is transferred by conveyor belt to the wooden dump wagon alongside.

CAROLINE ODEN SEPULVEDA

1924. *Caroline Oden (Mrs. Roman D.) Sepulveda cuddles her first great grandchild Andrew Suich with obvious pleasure.*

EARLY 1920s. *Longshoremen in white hats stand in front of a parade float depicting the* S.S. SAN PEDRO. *The I.L.A. No. 38-18 was chartered around 1908 but proved rather ineffective during the "open shop" days of San Pedro. After the 1923 maritime strike, unions were forced to retreat into a decade of inactivity. The National Recovery Act of 1933 provided the right of workers to organize.*

Averill Park lies near the western border of San Pedro's Vista del Oro residential area. Averill Canyon cuts across this ten-acre preserve, which was donated to the City of Los Angeles in 1920 by the Averill–Weymouth Company, developers of the district. Youngsters enjoy endless hours endeavoring to catch the elusive crawdads and mosquito fish found in the series of terraced pools fed by a cascading brook and miniature waterfall.

CIRCA 1920s. *White Point viewed from the west shows the sulphur springs spa and hotel on the beach. The access road (center) is in good repair. A cluster of houses on the bluff to the left forms the colony of the White Point Japanese dry farmers, who cultivated the hillside acreage with remarkable success.*

DON ROMAN SEPULVEDA

1927. *Don Roman Sepulveda, at age seventy-three, is seated ramrod straight on one of his favorite steeds. Aside from establishing the first water works in San Pedro, Don Roman was instrumental in the construction of the White Point spa; an organizer of the First National Bank; county supervisor of roads; member of the City of San Pedro Board of Trustees and developer of the Carolina, Grand View and Sepulveda Tracts.*

1925. *Point Fermin Lighthouse on the cliff in the background is viewed from the Wilder Addition of Point Fermin Park. The pergolas are still popular for picnics and summer evening suppers.*

CIRCA 1925. *The U.S. Navy or Twenty-second Street Landing is shown at its Outer Harbor location. The Pacific Electric car line was extended to this point so that sailors might depart directly for Los Angeles, Long Beach or other destinations. In this manner the temptations offered near the Fifth Street Landing, adjacent to Beacon Street bars, were avoided — at least in theory.*

1924. *Public memorial services were held for the sailors killed in a turret explosion of the U.S.S. MISSISSIPPI. The massing of the sailors for the fleet was at Trona Field (later called Navy Field) located east of Pacific Avenue and just south of the old Trona Plant. This area was incorporated into the Middle Reservation of Fort MacArthur when it expanded south towards Stephen M. White Drive in the late 1930s.*

U.S. NAVY LANDING
OUTER HARBOR-
SAN PEDRO, CALIF.

IN MEMORIUM
U.S.S. MISSISSIPPI — JUNE 17-1924.

Crowds view one of the two four-teen–inch railroad guns brought to Fort MacArthur by 1926. Only four of these "Big Berthas" were pro-duced, two being shipped to the Philippines. More than three mil-lion people observed this weapon during the course of its trip from Aberdeen Proving Grounds, Mary-land — 60,000 of them in Los An-geles alone. Practice firing of the artillery resulted in extensive win-dow breakage, subsequent damage claims and complaints. The outmod-ed weapons were dismantled during the 1940s.

absorbed by Los Angeles. Between July and September, 1919, the Dodson, Fort MacArthur, Peck and Harbor View Tracts were an-nexed, increasing the area of the San Pedro district by 2.2 square miles, almost half again what it had been at consolidation. Later, the Hamilton and White Point additions in 1925 and 1928, respec-tively, together added another 289 acres. Fortunately for the people, early developers had a sense of community, as the many parks in San Pedro attest, since most of them are on donated land. Some bear names that honor the benefactors: Peck Park for George H. Peck; Leland, Rena and Alma Parks for Peck's son and daughters; Averill Park for Herbert O. Averill, who with his brother-in-law, H.L. Weymouth, developed the Vista del Oro area; and the Wilder Addition of Point Fermin Park for Charles T. Wilder, Peck's adopted nephew. In Wilmington the Banning family donated their mansion and adjacent land for public park use. Today, these are the General Phineas T. Banning Residence Museum and Ban-ning Park.

1925. The Pacific Fleet lies at an-chor inside the breakwater. In the foreground is Pedro Point, which was later to become Cabrillo Beach.

A SECTION OF THE BUSINESS DISTRICT OF SAN PEDRO & THE GREAT INNER HARBOR LOOKING N. FR.

1925. *Looking north toward West Basin, one sees Boschke Slough in the foreground and to the right the Kerckhoff-Cuzner Mill and Lumber Company. At upper center is Todd Shipyard, originally the Los Angeles Shipbuilding and Drydock Company, established in 1917. Due north across the channel, the white tanks of the Associated Oil Company (now Getty Oil Company) adjoins the new San Pedro Lumber Company site.*

In the years following World War I, tonnage handled by the port steadily increased, rising from 2.2 million tons in fiscal 1917–18 to 26.5 million tons in 1923–24, when Los Angeles surpassed all other West Coast ports in tonnage handled. (That leadership position was maintained every year until 1974, when Long Beach handled more tonnage.) In 1925 seventy percent of the 13.7 million tons that passed through the Panama Canal originated in or was destined for the Port of Los Angeles. That year civic boosters claimed a population of over 30,000 people for San Pedro.

Port development kept pace all through the twenties. The Badger Avenue (now Henry Ford Avenue) Bascule Bridge over

AIR VIEW OF CHANNEL AND DOCKS SAN PEDRO, CAL. 188

THE NEW DODSON THEATRE BLDG

Cerritos Channel was constructed and a concrete viaduct down the bluff to the Outer Harbor terminals replaced the wooden one. A second fireboat went into operation in 1925. Designated Fireboat No. 2,* it is still in service and docks at Berth 227 on Terminal Island, where Firehouse No. 112* (a huge boathouse) was built in 1927. The original Fireboat No. 1, a large tug-type vessel that had entered service in 1919, was replaced by a smaller, modern type in 1968. Extensive dredging operations improved the West Basin and widened the entrance channel to 1,000 feet. By the end of 1926, there were 33,785 feet of municipal wharves, 24,335 feet of private wharves and a railroad belt line inaugurated to consolidate all railroad facilities at the port. In 1928, 7,532 vessels entered the harbor and over twenty-five million tons of cargo were handled. Practically all channels were at a depth of thirty-five feet.

*Both fireboat and firehouse are designated as Los Angeles City Historic-Cultural Monument No. 154.

1924. *This view is to the northeast from the new Fox Cabrillo Theatre. At the extreme left are the First National Bank and the Globe Theatre at Sixth and Palos Verdes Streets. Midway toward the old domed City Hall is the clock-towered Bank of San Pedro. The Carnegie Library (center front) served as a library beginning in 1906, but during World War II it functioned as the Chamber of Commerce office and the Rationing Board. The steamer and sailing vessel are unloading lumber at the Southern Pacific tie wharf. At far right is the site that ultimately became Ports O'Call. The Main Channel is in the process of being widened to 1,000 feet and Terminal Island is being enlarged with the resultant dredger "spoil."*

1925. *The St. Francis Hotel stood near the intersection of Fifth and Palos Verdes Streets. Once considered the best family hotel in town, it is shown being reset after extensive road grading. This site now serves as the Pacific Trade Center parking lot. Fifth Street Elementary School is seen at far right background above Centre Street. This brick structure which succeeded the original school was razed in 1930.*

1925. *The Hotel Maryland still stands between Grand and Pacific Avenues on Eighth Street.*

1925. *The First National Bank was located on the southwest corner of Sixth and Palos Verdes Streets across from the old Globe Theatre.*

1925. *This building housing the Barton Hill Public Market has gone through various changes. During the 1930s it became Fitzsimmons Market and today serves the Barton Hill community as a laundromat. Two doors to the right is the former Barton Hill Theatre, which has also served as a church and today is a dance school. Goebel's Cafe, renowned for its hamburgers, was next door to the cinema.*

1926. The Army-Navy YMCA was built as a hotel and recreation center for servicemen at Ninth and Beacon Streets. Gradually it began to serve the need for swimming and public meeting room facilities for the community-at-large. The hotel rooms were a haven for young travelers and the elderly until new modern YMCA quarters were constructed in 1966. Since then the premises have been occupied by Harbor View House, a mental health hostel. Los Angeles Historic-Cultural Monument No. 252.

The present Fifteenth Street School replaced the original structure that burned down in 1922. In the mid-1960s cosmetic changes were made when the buildings were reinforced to comply with the earthquake code.

1929. Mrs. Belle Maloy Quinn stands by her Packard Town Sedan parked in front of the Quinn residence at 209 North Hanford. This home is now the convent of the Sisters of the Presentation, B.V.M., who serve the Parish of Holy Trinity (Roman Catholic) Church.

1926. *The first Barton Hill Elementary School (no longer standing) was built before 1909 on Pacific Avenue north of O'Farrell Street. It is seen here surrounded by the or-nate 1917 structures, which were later stuccoed, modernized and reinforced to conform with safety codes after the 1933 earthquake.*

1927. *The team ferry* T.F. *is being towed by the tug* OTTER *after a breakdown. This ferry service operated from 1914 to 1940 between First Street in San Pedro and Terminal Island.*

All this shipping activity was a boon to the Beacon Street business district. Pacific Avenue and Sixth Street were also becoming important commercial streets as more businesses opened along them. The San Pedro Municipal Building on Seventh and Beacon was dedicated in 1928. This was the last major municipal facility to be erected in the Harbor District for many years to come.

During the period from 1900 through the 1920s, the ethnic makeup of the Harbor Area became established. The development of Fish Harbor and its associated maritime industries attracted Portuguese, Scandinavians and Greeks. The Portuguese had been represented in the area from the 1850s when the California gray whale had become the prey of whalers. Japanese created a community on Terminal Island and for a time dominated the fishing indus-

1928. Harbor Boulevard is viewed toward the north with the San Pedro Municipal Building ("City Hall") under construction. The latter is located in the traditional heart of San Pedro at Seventh and Beacon Streets. To the left is the Carnegie Library, built in 1906 and demolished about 1966.

1928. The finale of Nob Hill before being leveled, with the Hotel San Pedro (originally the Clarence) making its last stand. Reduced in size and grandeur, the structure was lowered to street level and served as a work- *ing person's hotel until burned for fire practice during the 1940s. This view from Berth 90 shows Pacific Electric cars in the foreground. In the far right background the Robal Inn (1917) can be seen.*

try. Discovery of vast schools of Pacific sardines and tuna in near-by waters attracted Adriatic and Mediterranean Yugoslavs (primarily from the Dalmatian Islands) and Italians (principally from Southern Italy) to join their pioneer countrymen of the eighties. All of these immigrants and the native Mexican population created the rich diversity of cultures that characterizes the Harbor Area.

Dredging and filling operations to create Reservation Point on the south end of Terminal Island were started in 1927. Removal of Deadman's Island was part of this federal project and demolition of the island was finally completed in 1929. Its existence had been considered a hazard to navigation and the removal widened the entrance channel. With its destruction a landmark that had identified the harbor from its earliest days disappeared. This project marked the end of a thirty-year period of harbor improvement and vigorous economic growth that created the largest man-made harbor on the West Coast. Then the bubble burst and the nation fell into the devastating worldwide economic depression. The year 1929 ended on a sour note.

1928. Over the years San Pedro High School has produced many great baseball teams. The Honorable Vincent Thomas, assemblyman for thirty–eight years and late dean of the California Assembly, is crouched in the second row, third from the right.

MARCH 20, 1927. *Members of the Italian Mutual Benefit Society were organized by Antonio Streva in 1925 as Mazzini Lodge No. 1 (named for the nineteenth-century Italian patriot Giuseppi Mazzini). The impetus of the group was to assist with the Americanization of Italian immigrants, encourage civic involvements and provide social activities.*

CIRCA 1928. *Rudecinda Crypt, located in Harbor View Memorial Park, is the burial place for many members of the Sepulveda and Dodson families. (See inside front cover, no. 1.)*

5

DEPRESSION
AND WAR

Los ANGELES dangled the communities of San Pedro and Wilmington on the end of a political umbilical cord called the Shoestring Strip which made them contiguous parts of the city. The City Hall was twenty-five miles away and by 1930 it was a fair question in which direction the economic benefits of consolidation flowed more strongly. The last of the harbor improvement bonds had been floated some time earlier and subsequent improvements were funded by port revenues and federal appropriations. The city treasury, however, was still enjoying revenues collected in the harbor communities. No one fussed much over this until the depression took hold and the crunch was felt.

In the early thirties the urban sprawl we know today had not yet begun. A vast stretch of farmland separated San Pedro and

Opposite page: **1932. Life during the depression years in San Pedro was often enlivened by visiting one of the cinemas in town. The Fox Cabrillo Theatre, near the intersection of Seventh and Palos Verdes Streets, was a favorite meeting place of the younger generation. Offices and businesses surrounding the theatre included Painless Parker Dentist, above the corner soda fountain, and Western Union a few doors east.**

CIRCA **1935. A patriotic parade crosses Seventh Street while marching south on Pacific Avenue.**

The March 10, 1933, earthquake caused considerable damage in the Beacon Street and downtown area. Bricks fell from many buildings including the Southern Counties Gas Company at Seventh and Centre Streets.

From 1910 to 1924 the Industrial Workers of the World were a source of agitation against the Establishment, which was supportive of open shop conditions. This advertisement typifies the I.W.W. appeal to the working class who were consistently exhorted by such newspapers as the LOS ANGELES TIMES *about where their loyalties should lie under the free enterprise system.*

Wilmington from the urban center of Los Angeles. The connecting Shoestring Strip was also mostly farmland. Thus insulated from the city proper, San Pedro and Wilmington retained their own distinctive characters. The 1930 census counted 35,918 people in San Pedro and 14,907 in Wilmington. Very likely most of them had to think twice to remember that they were part of the larger city.

As everywhere else in the nation, the Harbor District suffered from the depression. Thousands became jobless as shipping activity slowed and shipyards became idle. Only a few found employment from the limited harbor improvements that were undertaken. Warehouses were built on the landfill north of the Twenty-second Street extension in 1931 and work was begun on the outer basin of Fish Harbor. In the next year work was begun on the federally funded 12,500-foot middle breakwater.

The Long Beach earthquake hit the Harbor District in 1933, tumbling brick facades and breaking windows throughout the San Pedro Bay area. San Pedro High School suffered structural damage and harbor property damage was estimated at $250,000. Construction of a new high school at Fifteenth and Alma Streets was soon begun and the school was opened for classes in the fall of 1936.

There was strong labor activity in all the West Coast ports during this period. The movement in Los Angeles Harbor had its beginning in the latter years of the last century and grew to formidable proportions during World War I. After the war, however, anti-labor elements combined to nullify union gains and succeeded in having wartime concessions to labor revoked. The militant "Wobblies" (Industrial Workers of the World) made an impact on the waterfront through their Marine Transport Workers Industrial Union No. 510 by striking and tying up the docks for several days

Downtown San Pedro received a drastic "haircut" as a result of the 1933 earthquake when all cornices, ornamentation and the Bank of San Pedro's clock tower were ordered removed in the interest of public safety.

in 1923. Lacking support from the larger Seaman's Union, which did not share the radical philosophy of the Wobblies, the strike failed. The open shop, with the company-controlled Sea Service Bureau operating the hiring halls, became the rule on the waterfront. Many of the Wobblies' leadership were arrested and jailed under the Criminal Syndicalist Law legislated in reaction to the "Red Scare" that influenced much of the political thinking of the post-World War I period.

Though the dockworkers' union had been "busted," the labor movement was not dead and workers eventually reorganized as

1934. This east view of the central business district at Sixth Street and Pacific Avenue shows the P.E. (Pacific Electric) car overhead wires and tracks. At the left is the Art Deco Warner Brothers Theatre. Los Angeles Historic-Cultural Monument No. 251.

1930. Anderson Memorial at Ninth and Mesa Streets was built in 1925 for youth activities. It was dedicated to the memory of Mr. and Mrs. N.O. Anderson's two sons, who died during the influenza epidemic of 1918. The plunge was a popular attraction until earthquake damage necessitated its removal in the late 1930s. In more recent years the structure was converted to the Senior Citizens Recreation Center.

The present San Pedro High School on Fifteenth between Meyler and Leland Streets was opened in 1936. The well-known architect George Kaufman designed this building, the Los Angeles Times Building and many other important structures.

part of the International Longshoreman's Association (I.L.A.). In 1934 the West Coast was disrupted by an I.L.A.-led general strike. After failing to tie up shipping in the harbor by peaceful picketing, 300 union longshoremen stormed Berth 143 in Wilmington and set fire to a strikebreakers' stockade. In the melee that followed, six strikers were shot, two fatally, and a number of strikebreakers were clubbed. California Governor James Rolph, Jr., appealed to President Franklin D. Roosevelt to establish an arbitration board to settle the strike. Union and employer negotiators agreed to

1935. *The Federal Building, which houses the U.S. Post Office, is located on Beacon between Eighth and Ninth Streets. This building is representative of what is sometimes referred to as Public Works Administration moderne, a sort of conservative or classicized Art Deco, and is considered one of the best examples of this type of architecture. Of particular interest is a forty-foot mural by Fletcher Martin in the lobby. The U.S. Custom Service formerly maintained offices here.*

CIRCA 1930. *Richard Henry Dana Junior High School was named in honor of the voyager and author of* TWO YEARS BEFORE THE MAST. *Dana came ashore from the brig* PILGRIM *on which he served as an ordinary seaman. Hides stored in the Casa de San Pedro were boated out to the ship anchored well offshore. The exterior of the school was altered in recent years to comply with the earthquake safety code.*

submit the issues to the panel. After four months of extensive investigation, the arbitrators awarded labor significant concessions, among them: joint control of the hiring halls, outlawing of the employers' blacklist, a six-hour day, a grievance procedure plus wage and working-hour adjustments.

Economic recovery was slow and federal projects continued to provide employment for many. A Federal Building, housing the Post Office, Customs and other services, was constructed at Beacon and Ninth Streets in 1935. The Custom House was eventually

1933. *San Pedro is south of the Union Oil Refinery complex. Note the undeveloped parts of West Basin in the foreground.*

EARLY-TO-MID 1930s. *A sizeable section of land at Point Fermin along Paseo del Mar began to slide seaward in 1929. Maximum movement was eleven inches per day. By quick action all except two homes on the seaward side of the street were moved to solid ground. The eastern section of the park was lost and the entire area remains unstable though stationary at present. Referred to as a "slump," geologists regard it as an outstanding example and have featured this phenomenon in many books.*

In 1940 Vincent Thomas, who had become a San Pedro resident in 1924, ran against the political establishment for the California Assembly on a platform of secession from Los Angeles. With a campaign cry of "I hate Los Angeles," he was overwhelmingly elected and went on to serve for thirty-eight years, longer than any assemblyman in the state's history. In a March 20, 1979, article, the Los Angeles *Herald-Examiner* quoted Thomas as saying that, if given the opportunity, the citizens of San Pedro would vote to secede from the City of Los Angeles. Secession is an ever-recurring subject of conversation in San Pedro.

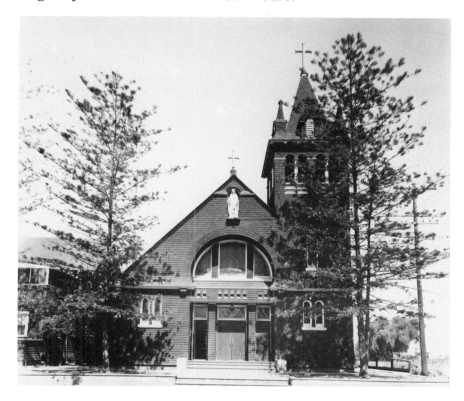

Parishioners of Mary Star of the Sea Catholic Church constructed their second church building on the corner of Ninth and Centre Streets in 1905. New church facilities were built at Seventh and Meyler Streets and shortly afterward this facility was demolished, even though efforts had been made to insure its preservation.

Stucco homes in many styles were fashionable in the late twenties and thirties. They were located in various parts of the community, especially in the Vista del Oro area.

1935. *View from the hill above Stephen White Drive shows the breakwater, Cabrillo Beach, the boat and bath houses, and the picnic shelters. Apartment buildings are now located on the open area in the foreground.*

The Japanese air attack on Pearl Harbor on December 7, 1941, brought the United States into World War II. Within days the war came to San Pedro when the steamship *Absaroka* was damaged by torpedoes off Point Fermin. Before December was over the Japanese submarine *I-35* was spotted on the surface off the Palos Verdes Peninsula and sunk by American aircraft. The navy took over control of ship operations in the harbor and the army set up anti-aircraft guns at Lookout Point on Gaffey Street between Thirty-fourth and Thirty-sixth Streets. (The concrete pedestals on which the guns were mounted still remain, but with telescopes for

This scene depicts the "calm side" inner beach and the boathouse pier that extended east about 100 yards to a float at the end. The beach has been a favorite San Pedro recreation area since the 1920s.

Los Angeles Harbor Light was un-officially designated Angel's Gate Lighthouse after a "gate" was created by completion of the Federal Breakwater extension (circa 1937). The tower was activated in 1913 with a powerful beacon and a diaphone fog signal, which became known as "Moaning Maggie." In the interest of economy, Maggie's two-tone signal gave way to a type of "fish horn."

1935. The Yugoslav community in San Pedro is regarded as the most important of such settlements on the West Coast. These pioneers of the fishing industry constructed their hall at Seventeenth and Palos Verdes Streets. The ground–breaking ceremony is shown here. The clubhouse is still the center for their various social activities.

1940s. *During World War II oil tanks in the Harbor Area were camouflaged to avoid aerial detection by the enemy.*

CIRCA 1940. *This comprehensive aerial view shows the limits of the city at Western Avenue. Beyond that, the open fields and hills are unpopulated except for the small group of homes known as Miraleste (center background). Note the Globe A-1 grain elevator just south of the Ferry Building.*

sightseers.) The Harbor District mobilized for the war. Shipyards began producing at full capacity and an estimated 20,000 more people poured into the area to do their part for the war effort.

Among the many tragedies brought about by the war was the disbandment of the two communities that had developed on Terminal Island. The small community of East San Pedro grew out of the labor camps set up on the island during construction of the breakwater to Deadman's Island in the 1870s. When the Los Angeles Terminal Railway later acquired the island, another rail link between Los Angeles and a deepwater terminal was established. They also developed a seaside resort, and before the modern breakwaters were completed, the ocean surf broke on the curving east side of the island. Here was Brighton Beach, a popular turn–of–the–century playground and a fashionable place to own a summer home. But as land reclamation projects encroached and fish canneries were built nearby, the area became less attractive as a resort and the leisure crowd was eventually displaced by the working class. As the years passed the community, now known as Terminal, developed into a modest working-class neighborhood that stretched along the spine of the island. Landfill operations left Brighton Beach high and dry, with the nearest open water almost a mile away.

MID-1940s. *The first drive-in restaurant in San Pedro was established at the corner of Sixth and Gaffey Streets. As elsewhere in the nation, this innovation proved to be a very popular attraction and convenience for all age groups.*

The other community on the island grew on the landfill that created Fish Harbor and retained the name of East San Pedro. Unlike Terminal, where Europeans, Mexicans, Filipinos and Japanese lived in a multi-ethnic community, East San Pedro developed principally as a Japanese community. It had its beginnings in the early 1900s, when fishermen built squatter shacks on the first breakwater that extended to Deadman's Island and moored their boats below their shacks. Some of them had been fishermen in Japan and they brought their skills to the budding fishing industry. The construction of Fish Harbor in 1916 provided sites for

MID-1940s. *Looking southeast, Barton Hill School is visible at lower right. Rancho San Pedro Housing Project can be seen at center left, with the "City Hall," Post Office and YMCA (now Harbor View House) at center background. To the right of the Main Channel stands Warehouse No. 1. Angel's Gate Lighthouse sits at the far end of the Federal Breakwater that extends from Cabrillo Beach.*

CIRCA 1930. *The Buddist Temple in East San Pedro, the southern section of Terminal Island, provided an artistic contrast to the severely plain fishing colony houses adjacent to the canneries at Fish Harbor.*

1944. *Channel Heights, an award winning World War II low-cost housing development, was designed by the celebrated architect Richard Neutra. The project's practical layout made it particularly noteworthy. The units bordered on Western Avenue and overlooked North Gaffey Street, which in the mid–nineteenth century was the Sepulveda stage route. In the distance on the opposite hill, an array of tanks indicates the scope of the Union Oil Company's activities in the Harbor Area. The white patches indicate Western Terrace, a housing development on the site of the old Suang-na Indian village. The wartime housing projects have been replaced in recent times by modern mid-income residences and condominiums, the Los Angeles Police Department facility and the extension of the Harbor Freeway.*

canneries and a location for the growing Japanese community. The new harbor was a safe anchorage for the fishing boats and the canneries built modest homes that the Japanese rented. A business district grew as stores and restaurants opened on Tuna Street between Wharf Street and Terminal Way. The school district opened a branch of the Terminal Elementary School to serve the community. With little to connect it with Terminal, almost a mile to the north, East San Pedro developed in relative isolation and might have been a town transplanted directly from Japan.

The destruction by fire of the Japanese fishing camp at Port Los Angeles on Santa Monica Bay resulted in an influx of new people in 1917–18. Later, other Japanese transferred operations from Monterey to take advantage of Southern California's longer

1945. *Beatrix Hessova painted this watercolor of Saint Margaret's Chapel, which was on the Gaffey estate in the area of the present-day YMCA. Originally constructed in 1913 as a playhouse for Margaret Gaffey, it later served as the chapel for her marriage. Funeral services for her father, John Gaffey, were also conducted within the twenty-by-twenty-five foot adobe, brick and plaster building.*

fishing season. Los Angeles Harbor became the world's leading fishing industry center largely as a result of the fishing fleet (composed of thirty percent Japanese, twenty percent Yugoslavs, seven percent Italians and the remaining forty-three percent other national groups) based here. In the 1930s over 2,000 Japanese lived in East San Pedro, with more than sixty stores and shops, doctors, a dentist, a post office branch, a bank and a newspaper.

Though hard hit by the depression, the community held together until the economic situation had eased. But then came the war and the Japanese were classed as enemy aliens. In 1942 the Japanese of East San Pedro and elsewhere in the Harbor District were forced from their homes and transported to relocation camps with only such meager possessions as could fill the two suitcases allowed each person. The community of Terminal was also condemned and all the residents were required to vacate. Today, Terminal Island is devoted solely to port and industrial activities.

1944. *The hill above Western Avenue (then only two lanes wide) affords an overview of Peck Park. George Peck bought this land, as well as much of the surrounding area, from Aurelio Sepulveda and started to develop this tract in the early 1920s.*

1941 OR 1942. *Fort MacArthur's Lower Reservation or "Bottom Side" was a World War II installation built on landfill below and east of the main post during the late 1930s. During the war these buildings housed the many draftees processed at this installation and contained such facilities as the commissary and the post exchange. This is the site of a new marina, part of the West Channel Cabrillo Beach Recreational Complex. Twenty-second Street is in the foreground and the large open area that abuts Pacific Avenue at upper right is the Parade Ground.*

1944. *The barren soil in the foreground is a bleak reminder of land previously tilled by Japanese farmers interned during the spring of 1942. At center, Summerland Avenue terminates at Western, which was then the edge of town.*

The military took over White Point and the hotel, restaurant, salt water plunge and Don Roman's little house were demolished. The beautiful palm trees and hanging gardens fell to the ravages of neglect. Socials in front of the cliffside fireplace — as they had been known in the prewar decades — never returned to the White Point cove. It was the end of an era.

The Harbor District became the scene of unrelenting activity during those war years. Ships crowded the harbor and the shipyards were busy around the clock. Fort MacArthur bulged with inductees, introducing over 750,000 civilians to the rigors of

1948. *Aerial view looking north from the Union Oil Company of California refinery shows Harbor Lake (formerly Machado Lake or Bixby Slough) at top center background.* *At upper left is the U.S. Navy quonset–hut wartime housing and the three-sided 76 sign looms on this side of Gaffey Street.*

military life. Soldiers and sailors crowded San Pedro's streets and the district around Beacon Street became more notorious than ever.

Finally, the war ended in the summer of 1945 and demobilization began on a massive scale. Defense contracts were cancelled and shipyards laid off thousands of workers. The navy relinquished its control over shipping operations in the port and the harbor quickly returned to its peacetime patterns.

1945. *Todd Shipyard Corporation, originally established in 1917 as the Los Angeles Shipbuilding and Drydock Company, is shown geared for World War II production. The massive gantry crane installation at the building ways was designed to facilitate construction of large ships.*

JANUARY 11, 1949. *Like a scene from a Currier and Ives print, the Palos Verdes Hills and San Pedro are blanketed in snow. Such sights are indeed rare in the Harbor Area.*

The war did not displace Los Angeles as the world's leading fishing port. In 1947 fishing boats began berthing in the Southern Pacific slip at Berth 73. Fish market operations were moved to Berth 72 from the condemned structure at Berth 80, and in 1951 the new Municipal Wholesale Fish Market at the foot of Twenty-second Street was completed.

Passenger traffic was also a major activity in the port. In 1950 the most modern postwar passenger-cargo terminal was dedicated for American President Lines (APL) at Berths 153–155 in Wilmington and work was started on a new marine terminal at Wilmington Berths 195–198 for Matson Navigation Company. The war was left behind and commerce came to dominate harbor activities once again.

Opposite page: **In preparation for a fishing trip, sturdy fishermen are loading their mended nets aboard a purse seiner docked at Fish Slip. Across the way lies an identical example of such vessels.**

6

MODERN
SAN PEDRO

SAN PEDRO entered the fifties with a population of 53,578. All indications were that growth would continue in the decades to come. Zoning ordinances adopted in 1946 anticipated a population of 240,000 by 1990. With the postwar population explosion taking place in Southern California, few doubted this projection. Developers began building homes in tracts along the Palisades and on the hillside east and west of today's Western Avenue, just south of Ninth Street and on the north side of town, respectively. Unlike earlier arrivals, however, the new residents were coming to San Pedro not for employment but for a desirable community to live in. San Pedro was becoming a bedroom community.

With the outbreak of the Korean War in June, 1950, Fort MacArthur was revived from its caretaker status. The artillery and mortars that were its initial reason for existence had been removed from their emplacements and scrapped at the end of World War II; the post became an Army Reserve Training Center. In the fifties with Cold War tensions increasing, Nike missile sites were constructed to defend metropolitan centers around the country from enemy missiles. Fort MacArthur became the air defense headquarters for Southern California.

By the late 1960s air defense requirements had changed and in the early seventies the Defense Department declared Fort MacArthur surplus property. Many in the community protested the fort's closing and its impact on the local economy. Nevertheless, in 1976 the Lower Reservation below the bluff was turned over to the Los Angeles Harbor Department, while Upper Reservation land was transferred to the Los Angeles Department of Recreation and Parks and to the Los Angeles Unified School District. Army Reserve activities were moved to Los Alamitos in 1979. All formal army operations were terminated except for a caretaker detachment. Only the California National Guard continued to use the Middle Reservation, mainly during the week

VINCENT THOMAS

Vincent Thomas, late dean of the California Assembly, was honored for his long years of service and ardent support of harbor interests by having the bridge named after him.

Opposite page: 1962. Shown is the stringing of the first two cables of the Vincent Thomas Bridge. From these the entire web evolved for the "bridge to nowhere," which has developed into one of the harbor's most vital arteries since opening in 1963.

A slippery load of mackerel is piled on the deck of a purse-seine fishing boat docked at the cannery wharf. Note the box of select larger fish, apparently reserved for family, friends, crew's dinners or possibly the fresh market.

Below: **1950.** *Longshoremen "belly–pack" banana stalks to the conveyor belt. These stems varied in size and weight, sometimes exceeding 100 pounds. This handling method was discontinued in 1965 and the fruit now comes packed in forty-pound boxes. Since then, damage has been considerably reduced.*

Opposite page, top: **EARLY 1950s.** *The former Saint Peter's Episcopal Church (1884) paused in the intersection of Sixth Street and Harbor Boulevard as it traveled a circuitous route from Tenth and Mesa Streets to its present site in Harbor View Cemetery at Twenty-fourth Street and Grand Avenue, where it now serves as a chapel.*

Opposite page, bottom: **CIRCA 1950s.** *This is looking north on Western Avenue. At the left is the road leading to the Hacienda Hotel and Golf Course, a community financed venture designed to provide San Pedro with first-class accommodations suitable for conventions and important functions. The hotel was later demolished and a condominium complex constructed in its place. At right in the distance is the intersection of First Street and Western Avenue.*

ends. The community remains keenly interested in the ultimate fate of the fort.*

The decade of the fifties saw extensive improvements in port facilities to accommodate changing patterns in shipping. The new passenger terminals for Matson and American President Lines (APL) were completed and contracts were let for the construction of the Consolidated Marine, Inc. (CMI) Terminal at Berths 87–93. The CMI Terminal was intended to consolidate all passenger traffic through the port and to handle the 1,400-passenger superliners expected to be built by APL. However, the superliners were never built. Instead, the popularity of passenger ships declined as more travelers opted for the speed of air travel. Bowing to economics, Matson and APL discontinued their once flourishing passenger services to the Hawaiian Islands, South Pacific and Far East. Completed in 1962, the CMI Terminal now provides passenger facilities for cruise ships, including the *Queen Elizabeth II* on her annual calls, and container facilities for APL.**

*On October 1, 1982, the army turned over the Middle Reservation east of Pacific Avenue to the U.S. Air Force, which has built family housing there. The property on the west side (site of the Army Hospital) had previously been sold to a private developer.

**Information released by the Harbor Department prior to publication indicates that APL will move to a new 100-acre terminal at Berths 121–126 in the West Basin. The CMI Terminal is now known as Eagle Marine and it will be converted to a full passenger terminal capable of handling up to five cruise ships at one time.

Though passenger traffic declined, other shipping activities increased. Oil has been an important product since 1911, when Union Oil Company of California laid the first pipeline to the port. In 1959 a supertanker terminal was built to handle the increasing volume of petroleum products passing through the harbor. The terminal connects with a ten-acre storage tank farm that had been erected earlier below the bluff north of Twenty-second Street, much to the chagrin of the Crescent Avenue homeowners on top of the bluff. By 1960 sixteen oil firms had facilities in the port with a combined storage capacity of nearly ten million barrels.

All through the fifties the Harbor Freeway was steadily extended south from Los Angeles. Finally reaching San Pedro, this high-speed traffic artery made the Harbor District more convenient for commuting and new residents were finding their way to San Pedro. Concern developed over the community's high growth rate and in 1962 a citizen planning committee drew up a general plan to guide the pattern of growth. The plan, which allowed for a 1990 population of 116,700, was never implemented because the zoning

The spherical oiltank lends itself to portraying a jack-o'-lantern. So annually during the Halloween season, Union Oil Company of California thrills trick or treaters by featuring the "Great Pumpkin" at its storage area on North Gaffey Street. Apples and caramel corn are distributed to small fry participating in this spooky event, while older folk reminisce of younger days.

*Opposite page: **The Harbor District's incinerator was an expensive experiment that was never fully utilized. Both this project and backyard incinerators were banned in the mid-1950s. Reactivation is being considered to assist in the endless battle against rubbish.***

On the bluff above the rocky shore was the site of the facilities of the San Pedro Golf and Country Club (circa 1927). Royal Palms, at the base of the cliff and just west of the ruins of White Point spa, was developed by Roman Sepulveda in the early twenties. The club sported an outdoor terrazzo tile dance floor and a native-stone fireplace where dances, barbecues and picnics were accommodated. The Palisades and South Shores are the developments along the hillside.

laws necessary to effectively guide such growth were never adopted by the City Council in faraway Los Angeles. However, one recommendation of the plan was adopted: urban renewal of the twelve-block area that became known as the Beacon Street Redevelopment District.

Long an area of unsavory reputation, the district had fallen victim to urban decay. Modern shipping methods had caused a sharp reduction in the number of seamen visiting the port. Tonnage for 1953–54 was 26.5 million, almost equal to that of 1928; yet only half the number of vessels were needed to carry that tonnage.

1955. Amity among the various religions in "melting pot" San Pedro is apparent at the Temple Beth-El Synagogue ground-breaking ceremonies. Reverend Lawrence Christensen, Pastor of Trinity Lutheran Church; Pietro DiCarlo, baker; Rabbi Wolli Kaelter, Temple Israel of Long Beach; Rabbi Leonard A. Helman, Temple Beth-El and Father John Wishard, Holy Trinity Church, stand ready with shovels to symbolically join in the traditional neighborliness of the varied faiths in the community.

Since then, ships have become even larger, crews smaller and the average length of stay reduced. The Beacon Street of ill-repute had no future. In 1969 the Los Angeles City Council approved the Beacon Street Redevelopment Project and demolition of the area's buildings followed soon after. Except for the housing originally planned for the north parcels, some commercial buildings on the west and some freshly paved streets crossing it, the area was "redeveloped" into nearly sixty acres of empty lots that remained vacant through most of the 1970s. Finally, during the last couple

CIRCA 1962. *Early construction on the Vincent Thomas Bridge is viewed from the San Pedro side as traffic travels along Harbor Boulevard at lower right. Signal Hill oil derricks, remnants of the sensational oil boom of the 1920s, are visible in the left background.*

1956. *Temple Beth-El and Center serves the local Jewish community. This edifice, which stands at Seventh Street and Averill Avenue, combines stained glass and Palos Verdes stone. It seats 400 for worship.*

1963. *This overview of the Main Channel looks north toward Wilmington from the main Post Office (Federal Building). Dominating the scene is the Vincent Thomas Bridge that is nearing completion. The ferry* ISLANDER *is approaching the San Pedro slip, while the smaller pedestrian ferry* ACE *lies alongside the public landing. The small ferries* ACE *and M.J.W. operated during rush periods and also between midnight and early morning hours when the* ISLANDER *was shut down. Ferry services were terminated simultaneously with the opening of the span.*

1963. *The completed Vincent Thomas Bridge spans the inner harbor. From center toward the right, note Consolidated Marine Incorporated (C.M.I.) on the threshold of containerization. This terminal occupies the former sites of "Mexican Hollywood" and the famous "Best American Beach" (B.A.B.), where skinny-dipping was the rule.*

of years of the decade, offices, shops, restaurants and a motel were constructed near Sixth and Beacon Street.

The last segment of the Harbor Freeway linked it with the Vincent Thomas Bridge to Terminal Island. Completed in 1963, the span of the bridge crosses the Main Channel 185 feet above the surface of the water. This was the first major suspension bridge erected in Southern California. On the day it opened to traffic, November 15, 1963, ferry service to Terminal Island was officially discontinued, further depressing Beacon Street business.

CIRCA 1965. *A former attraction at Ports O'Call was the old San Francisco ferryboat* SIERRA NEVADA, *built in 1913. This waterfront enterprise attracts sizeable crowds who wander through the old New England–type fishing village.*

Homer Toberman Settlement House was originated by the Methodist Women's Home Missionary Society in 1904 as a mission home and hospital in Los Angeles. Responding to changes in population and community needs, the organization moved to San Pedro in 1937. Over the past almost fifty years the facilities have grown from two bungalows to cover approximately one-third of a square block. Situated in a multi-ethnic neighborhood, it offers a diversity of programs pioneering both non-profit industry and neighborhood organizing.

The sixties saw many changes along the waterfront. Ports O'Call was developed on landfill that obliterated all signs of the old Southern Pacific Railroad wharf, built in the previous century. A bulk commodities terminal was constructed at Berth 49, Outer Harbor, adjacent to the supertanker terminal. The new $5 million Custom House was constructed on Terminal Island. Catalina Terminal was moved to Berths 95–96, in the shadow of the new bridge. The Canadian cruise ship *Princess Louise* was docked at Terminal Island across from Ports O'Call to begin life as a floating restaurant. (The *Louise* was moved to its present location at Berth 94 in 1979.) The stark framework of container cranes began to dominate the harbor skyline as more container terminals were constructed.

Preparations for the nation's 1976 Bicentennial had an impact on the Harbor District. These activities and the shock of the wholesale demolition of the Beacon Street district inspired many concerned residents to begin taking inventory of the community's historical and cultural heritage. The San Pedro Bay Historical Society was organized in 1974.

The Bicentennial brought the nation a gift of the Friendship Bell* from the Republic of Korea. This bell in its beautiful pagoda-like belfry stands on a hilltop above Point Fermin, visible for miles at sea. In 1976 the SS *Catalina*** did not carry passengers to Catalina Island as she had done in each of the previous fifty years. For a number of years the "Great White Steamship" had been unable to attract enough paying passengers to maintain economic viability and the ship made her last crossing in 1975. Beset by indebtedness, she was sold at auction in 1977. After three years as a veritable floating derelict, ravaged by neglect and vandals, she at last found a temporary haven inside the Long Beach breakwater. ☆

1970. The S.S. CATALINA, the "Great White Steamship," was built for William Wrigley in 1924 by the Los Angeles Shipbuilding and Dry Dock Company in San Pedro. Save for a tour of duty as a troop carrier on San Francisco Bay during World War II, the CATALINA served on the island run for about fifty years and established an enviable reputation for speed, comfort and safety.

In early 1977 work began on converting the old Ferry Building☆☆ into a maritime museum, which was opened to the public at the end of 1979. The USS *Los Angeles* (135) Naval Monument,★ dominated by the towering signal mast of that World War II heavy cruiser, stands in the small park in front of the Ferry Building. In Wilmington during 1977 the Banning Residence Museum unveiled a major exhibit of historic photos illustrating development of the port. The Officers Quarters of Drum Barracks was dedicated as a Civil War Museum in the fall of 1980.

Opposite page: 1971. Demolition of the buildings on Beacon Street was preceded by a celebration (wake) which lasted into the early morning hours with some of the old "hotspots" open for a final fling.

*Los Angeles City Historic-Cultural Monument No. 187.

**National Register of Historic Places, California Historical Landmark No. 894 and Los Angeles City Historic-Cultural Monument No. 213.

☆The San Pedro *News Pilot* of June 4, 1983, reported that the *Catalina* has been renovated and scheduled to begin carrying passengers to Avalon again.

☆☆Los Angeles City Historic-Cultural Monument No. 146.

★Los Angeles City Historic-Cultural Monument No. 188.

Last Night on Old Beacon Street

SAN PEDRO
SATURDAY, AUGUST 21st.

6 p.m. to ???

On The Street

DINING : DANCING : ENTERTAINMENT

4 HISTORIC BARS OPEN

MOVIE STARS WHO STARTED ON BEACON STREET ATTENDING

Following the celebration demolition will be underway - an era will pass into oblivion as the new day arrives for Beacon Street

USE FORM BELOW FOR TICKETS

TO   SAN PEDRO CHAMBER OF COMMERCE
390 WEST SEVENTH STREET, P.O. BOX 167
SAN PEDRO, CALIFORNIA 90733

LAST NIGHT ON OLD BEACON STREET

_____Tickets for International Dinner, Dancing, Entertainment @ $10 each . . . . . . $_____
(includes general admission)
_____Tickets for General Admission, Dancing, Entertainment @ $3 each . . . . . . $_____
Check Enclosed $_____

Circa 1970. *Looking north from the intersection of Seventh and Beacon Streets, the "City Hall" is situated on the right. On the northwest corner stands the A.P. Ferl Building, in which at one time the U.S. Custom House and Merchant Shipping Commission Office occupied the upstairs rooms. Part of the lower floor served as the main post office. The water tower, center background, is located at Todd Shipyard. This thoroughfare has since been eliminated between Fourth and Sixth Streets as part of the Beacon Street Redevelopment Project.*

1971. *Demolition of the Beacon Street complex deprived San Pedrans of a tangible link to its historic past. Tommy's Goodfellows Club, viewed in the midst of the rubble, was one of those establishments that ran through the short block and faced both Beacon and Front Streets.*

The issue of a liquid natural gas (LNG) terminal in the Port of Los Angeles was the subject of major controversy in the mid-seventies. A strong, vocal group of residents felt that such an installation would be a hazard to the community. Their fears were underscored when the oil tanker *Sansinena* exploded after discharging her cargo at the supertanker terminal. Five crewmen were killed, the terminal nearly destroyed and damage to the community though relatively minor was widespread. The incident seemed to solidify community opinion against an LNG terminal. Nevertheless, the

Los Angeles City Council voted in favor of locating such an installation in the port. None has yet been built and the gas companies have been investigating alternate sites.

This was not the first time people of the Harbor District protested the proposed actions of the established authorities. In 1964 the Harbor Department had advocated the construction of a marina at Cabrillo Beach, a favorite site for recurring pleasure-boat moorage proposals. This beach had been built up during the twenties by depositing sand on both sides of the breakwater where it

"Bye, Bye Beacon" was the theme for the Chamber of Commerce farewell party staged on the block between Fifth and Sixth Streets. Thereafter, demolition proceeded rapidly. The arched white-front building (center) is the former Alhambra Theatre and Hotel, which had been converted into a store. The dismantling revealed the old theatre seats, stage and fireproof curtain that had been floored over and walled in.

1980. The Beacon Street Redevelopment area looking northwest from the "City Hall." All buildings are newly completed or under construction except the Pacific Trade Center (1965) at upper left. The Harbor Department Building is being framed and immediately southeast of it is Bank of America. At center right is the Sunrise Motor Hotel, the rear of which occupies half of old Beacon Street.

1977. *Aerial view of the Palos Verdes Peninsula looking west shows the configuration of the Inner Harbor with Terminal Island in the foreground. The Point Fermin Headland is seen at far left and Point Vicente, seven miles up the coast, juts out at the western extremity. Unusual surf conditions sharply delineate the rugged coastline.*

joins the shore. The sand had been brought up from the bottom of the bay during channel-dredging operations. Determined community opposition to the loss of the beach had persuaded the Harbor Department to shelve those marina plans. Finally, the Harbor Department sponsored a citizen advisory committee to ensure community input to all phases of the planning and this resulted in the adoption of the marina development project* on the former Fort MacArthur Lower Reservation.

The beach was the center of another community controversy. In 1928 a bathhouse had been constructed at Cabrillo Beach and had been converted to a marine museum during the following decade. Subsequently, the Los Angeles Department of Recreation and Parks made plans for a new museum. In early 1975 the initial phase of construction began on a beach site south of the existing building. The project site aroused determined resistance in the community and the location was abandoned. The new Cabrillo Marine Museum was later constructed near the foot of the bluff. The ultimate fate of the old bathhouse is now in question.**

*By publication time, construction on the marina project was well under way with completion scheduled for the end of 1984.

**At publication time the Department of Recreation and Parks and the Southern California Oceanographic Studies Consortium, an association of six state universities, were actively pursuing a long-term lease agreement whereby the consortium would establish an oceanographic research center in the building.

Periodically during the seventies a proposal was made to construct an offshore airport on a man-made island in San Pedro Bay. Displaying an aversion to heavy air traffic and hordes of people streaming through their communities to and from the airport, the residents of the coastal cities and San Pedro organized in opposition and defeated the plan. Revived in the summer of 1980, the proposal was blocked again by strong, reawakened community opposition.

For three years a citizen advisory committee diligently worked on reviewing and updating the 1962 San Pedro Community Plan. On January 19, 1979, the group made its recommendations public at the first of a series of community meetings to solicit public comment prior to finalization of an updated plan. A moratorium on housing development in San Pedro was passed by the Los Angeles City Council in July, with some modification to the density provision recommended in the new plan. The moratorium that had been urged by a citizen committee was intended to control development until the Los Angeles Planning Commission could act on the plan, which projects a 1995 population of 92,000 and a population capacity of 105,000. (The 1980 census found 62,323 people in San Pedro and 45,070 in Wilmington.) Implementation of the new San Pedro Community Plan is a matter that requires approval of the Los Angeles City Council.*

*According to information received from the 15th Councilmanic District Office at publication time, the plan will become effective for different areas of the community as hearings are completed by the Planning Commission and action is taken by the City Council. In the meantime, a moratorium effective until February, 1984, requires that the zoning proposed in the plan be followed.

This twenty-five–by–fifty-foot mural, painted by Officer Abel Reynoso, depicts police history in the Harbor Area. This portrayal, highlighting many important landmarks of the area, is located at the Ryan Pitman Hall of the Harbor Division Pistol Range on North Gaffey Street. To the right of the Bank Cafe (left) is Captain C. G. Tenhausen, who headed the division beginning in 1914. Captain Robert A. McVey, area commanding officer, is at top center next to the Vincent Thomas Bridge.

The full moon adds to a spectacular night time view of the Korean Friendship Bell standing majestically at the southern end of Fort MacArthur's former Upper Reservation. The bell, weighing eighteen tons and the largest in the Western Hemisphere, was a gift "from the people of the Republic of Korea to the people of the United States" on the occasion of our Bicentennial in 1976.

The Harbor District enters the third century of the city's history facing challenging decisions. Now that so many of the area's residents are not directly dependent on the harbor for a living, it is no longer a case of "what's good for the port is good for the community." Perhaps a new chapter of this brief history will eventually be written to reexamine the events of the 1970s and carry the story into the eighties and beyond.

BIBLIOGRAPHY

Almeida, Arthur A. "San Pedro Waterfront Center of Post WW I Union Activity." San Pedro *Random Lengths,* no. 1 (1980).

—————. "White Point Sulphur Springs." *San Pedro Bay Historical Society Shoreline* 4, no. 5 (September, 1977).

Baker, Flora Twyman. "The Adobe Hidehouse at Old San Pedro — A One Hundred Year Saga." *San Pedro Bay Historical Society Shoreline* 4, no. 5 (September, 1977) and no. 6 (November, 1977).

Barsness, Richard W. *The Maritime Development of San Pedro Bay, California, 1821-1921.* Ph.D. dissertation, University of Minnesota, 1963.

Bell, Horace, Major. *Reminiscences of a Ranger.* Santa Barbara, Calif.: Wallace Hebberd, 1927.

Bigger, Richard and Kitchen, James D. *How the Cities Grew.* Los Angeles: Haynes Foundation, 1952.

Cleland, Robert Glass. *Cattle on a Thousand Hills, Southern California, 1850-1880.* San Marino, Calif.: Huntington Library, 1951.

Dakin, Susanna Bryant. *The Lives of William Hartnell.* Stanford, Calif.: Stanford University Press, 1949.

Dana, Richard Henry. *Two Years Before the Mast.* Los Angeles: Ward Ritchie Press, 1964.

Dumke, Glenn S. *The Boom of the Eighties.* San Marino, Calif.: Huntington Library, 1944.

Fink, Augusta. *Time and the Terraced Land.* Berkeley, Calif.: Howell-North Books, 1966.

Francis, Jessie Davis. *An Economic and Social History of Mexican California (1822-1846).* New York: Arno Press, 1976.

Gebhard, David and Winter, Robert A. *A Guide to Architecture in Los Angeles and Southern California.* Santa Barbara, Calif.: Peregrine Smith, Inc., 1977.

Gillingham, Robert Cameron. *The Rancho San Pedro.* Los Angeles: Dominguez Estate Co., 1961.

Govorchin, Gerald G. *Americans from Yugoslavia.* Gainesville, Fla.: University of Florida Press, 1961.

Grassman, Curtis. "The Los Angeles Free Harbor Controversy and the Creation of a Progressive Coalition." *Southern California Quarterly* 55, no. 4 (1973).

Grenier, Judson A., ed. *A Guide to Historic Places in Los Angeles County.* Dubuque, Iowa: Kendall/Hunt Publishing Co., 1978.

Guinn, J.M. *Historical and Biographical Record of Los Angeles and Vicinity.* Chicago: Chapman Publishing Co., 1902.

——————. *A History of California and an Extended History of Los Angeles and Environs.* Los Angeles: Historic Record Co., 1915.

——————. "The Lost Islands of San Pedro Bay." *Publications of the Historical Society of Southern California* 10 [1915–17].

Hager, Anna Marie and Everett Gordon. "San Pedro Proper Name for Gateway to World." San Pedro *News-Pilot,* Golden Anniversary Edition, 1959.

Historical Society of Southern California. "Padron de la Ciudad de Los Angeles y su Jurisdiccion (facsimile reproduction)." *Historical Society of Southern California Quarterly* 18, no. 3 (September–December, 1936).

Houston, John M. *Accounts and Stories of Old San Pedro.* Harbor City, Calif.: Economy Press, 1978.

Kawasaki, Kanichi. "The Japanese Community of East San Pedro, Terminal Island, California." Master's thesis, Dept. of Sociology, University of Southern California, 1931.

Krythe, Maymie. *Port Admiral: Phineas Banning, 1830-1885.* San Francisco: California Historical Society, 1957.

Layne, J. Gregg. "The First Census of the Los Angeles District." *Historical Society of Southern California Quarterly* 18, no. 3 (September–December, 1936).

Los Angeles Public Library, History Dept. Notebook. "Los Angeles and California Facts."

Lovrich, Nicholas P., Jr. *Yugoslavs and Italians in San Pedro: Political Culture and Civic Involvement.* Palo Alto, Calif.: Ragusan Press, 1977.

Ludwig, Ella A. *History of the Harbor District of Los Angeles.* [Los Angeles]: Historic Record Company [1927].

Mathes, W. Michael. *Vizcaino and Spanish Expansion in the Pacific Ocean 1580-1630.* San Francisco: California Historical Society, 1968.

Newmark, Harris. *Sixty Years in Southern California, 1853-1913.* 3rd ed. Boston: Houghton Mifflin Co., 1930.

Newmark, Maurice H. and Marco R. *Census of the City and County of Los Angeles, California, 1850.* Los Angeles: Times–Mirror Press, 1929.

Northrop, Marie E., ed. "The Los Angeles Padron Census of 1844, As Copied from the Los Angeles City Archives." *Historical Society of Southern California Quarterly* 42, no. 4 (December, 1960).

Ogden, Adele. "Hides and Tallow — McCulloch, Hartnell and Company, 1822-1828." *California Historical Society Quarterly* (1927).

Paez, Juan. *Cabrillo's Log, 1542-1543.* Translated by James R. Moriarity and Mary Keistmam. San Diego: Cabrillo Historical Association [1968].

Reps, John W. *Cities of the American West.* Princeton, N.J.: Princeton University Press, 1979.

Robinson, Alfred. *Life in California.* 1846. Reprint. New York: Da Capo Press, 1969.

Robinson, William Wilcox. *San Pedro and Wilmington.* Los Angeles: Title Guarantee and Trust Company, n.d.

—————. *Maps of Los Angeles.* Los Angeles: Dawson's Bookshop, 1966.

San Pedro Bay Historical Society Archives. "History of Los Angeles Harbor" by Donald A. Walsh.

Shirley, Christine F. V. "Entrepreneurs & Economics of the Los Angeles Shipping Industry." *California Historical Courier,* July, 1980.

Shotliff, Don A. "San Pedro Harbor, or Los Angeles Harbor?" *Southern California Quarterly* 54, no. 2 (Summer, 1972).

Thompson and West. *History of Los Angeles County, California.* 1880. Reprint. Berkeley, Calif.: Howell-North, 1959.

U.S. Bureau of the Census. *Ninth Census Population [1870].* Washington: Government Printing Office, 1872.

Vickery, Oliver. *Harbor Heritage.* [San Pedro, Calif., 1979.]

INDEX

COMPILED BY ANNA MARIE AND EVERETT GORDON HAGER

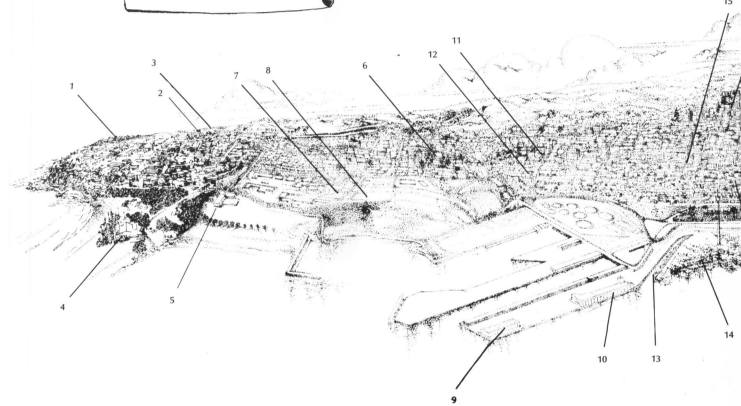

Drawing
of
San Pedro
by
Judy Ferguson
1983

1. **POINT FERMIN LIGHTHOUSE**
2. **KOREAN BELL**
3. **OSGOOD - FARLEY BATTERY (UPPER RES., FORT MAC ARTHUR)**
4. **CABRILLO BEACH BATHHOUSE**
5. **CABRILLO MARINE MUSEUM**
6. **HARBOR VIEW CEMETERY & ST. PETER'S CHURCH**
7. **FORT MAC ARTHUR (MIDDLE RES.)**
8. **HIDE HOUSE SITE**
9. **WAREHOUSE NO. 1**

10. **MUNICIPAL FISH MARKET**
11. **MULLER HOUSE**
12. **UNION ICE COMPANY**
13. **FISH SLIP**
14. **PORTS O'CALL**
15. **PECK HOUSE**
16. **DODSON HOUSE**